An Introduction to Programming and Algorithmic Reasoning using RAPTOR

By Steve Hadfield, Troy Weingart, and Wayne Brown

i

An Introduction to Programming and Algorithmic Reasoning using RAPTOR

by Steve Hadfield, Troy Weingart, and Wayne Brown
Department of Computer and Cyber Sciences
United States Air Force Academy

ISBN-13: 978-1987497724
ISBN-10: 1987497724

Published: April 2, 2018
Printed by CreateSpace, an Amazon.com Company

Preface

We wrote this text to introduce the cadets at the United States Air Force Academy to computer programming and algorithmic reasoning using the RAPTOR programming language and environment. At this point, we would like to share it with others who might find it useful.

RAPTOR is a graphical programming language based on flowcharts that are executable programs. RAPTOR minimizes syntax requirements so that the student can focus on the underlying logic and algorithmic reasoning required for computer programming. RAPTOR features built-in debugging aids including variable watches, break points, and instruction steps to aid in finding and correcting errors as well as verifying program correctness.

RAPTOR, which is an acronym for "Rapid Algorithmic ProtoTyping for Ordered Reasoning", was created by Terry A. Wilson, Martin C. Carlisle, Jeffrey W. Humphries, and Jason A. Moore. The RAPTOR programming language and environment can be downloaded free of charge from http://raptor.martincarlisle.com.

This text is sold just slightly above cost with any and all profits donated to Habitat for Humanity (https://www.habitat.org/).

Acknowledgments

We gratefully express our sincere appreciation to the many faculty members of the United States Air Force Academy's Department of Computer and Cyber Sciences who have provided invaluable insights and suggestions during the development and initial usage of this text as well as the thousands of cadets who have used early versions of this text for the Computer Science 110 – Introduction to Computing course.

RAPTOR Tutorial Videos

Dr. Randall Bower has created a series of RAPTOR tutorial videos aligned to the progression of this text. These videos are posted on YouTube and serve as an excellent learning aid. The topics and URLs to these videos are included below for your reference. They can also be easily found with a YouTube search on "raptor programming tutorial randallbower".

- Raptor 01 – Introduction   https://youtu.be/ZcAALK3movs
- Raptor 02 – Variables   https://youtu.be/eEoxssLPvkQ
- Raptor 03 – Files and Strings   https://youtu.be/8Qx2w2CDKrk
- Raptor 04 – Graphics   https://youtu.be/TW1rNIFzV-8
- Raptor 05 – Selection   https://youtu.be/vt7nyzxxylY
- Raptor 06 – Loops   https://youtu.be/_BTRJjFZY2Y
- Raptor 07 – Subcharts   https://youtu.be/TR2vm7XGL0o
- Raptor 08 – Animation   https://youtu.be/zCqZZkNDE9o
- Raptor 09 – Arrays   https://youtu.be/d2qlLvM4ijo

Table of Contents

1. An Introduction to Algorithmic Reasoning

What is Algorithmic Reasoning and Why is it Important?

Figure 1-1 - Apollo 13 Lift-Off (NASA Photo Gallery)

Figure 1-2 - Apollo 13 Crew (NASA Photo Gallery)

On April 11th, 1970, Apollo 13 lifted off from Cape Canaveral, Florida on humanity's third mission to land on the surface of the Moon. Enthusiasm ran high as Commander Jim Lovell, Command Module Pilot Jack Swigert, and Lunar Module Pilot Fred Haise sped across space. However, two days into the mission came those now famous words, "Houston, we have a problem." The explosion of an oxygen tank in the command module scrubbed the lunar landing and placed the crew's survival in serious jeopardy. The Apollo 13 crew was forced to move from the Command Module's accommodations for three to the Lunar Module that was designed for only two. As their return flight to earth progressed, carbon dioxide built up in the over-manned Lunar Module. Engineers on earth worked frantically to devise a means to build an 'air scrubber' to filter the carbon dioxide from the air using materials available in the spacecraft. These materials included a lithium hydroxide canister, charcoal filters, and parts of the astronauts' spacesuits. Once the engineers completed their fabrication of the air scrubber, they had to communicate directions on how to build the device to the very tired and cold space crew. For this, the engineers wrote a very clear and concise set of ordered steps by which the astronauts could build and then operate the air scrubber device. These instructions had to be correct, complete, unambiguous, and without omissions or contradictions. These instructions were an algorithm and they were developed with an intellectual skill called 'algorithmic reasoning'.

Figure 1-3 - Interior view of the Apollo 13 Lunar Module as the astronauts assemble a system to use the Command Module lithium hydroxide canisters to purge carbon dioxide from their air supply. (Turnill)

Obviously algorithms and algorithmic reasoning are important for rocket scientists and engineers; however algorithms and algorithmic reasoning are much more pervasive and fundamental to any human endeavor that involves developing step-by-step procedures for solving problems or accomplishing objectives. Furthermore, algorithms provide a critical means by which we can communicate processes for solving problems and accomplishing objectives to other people as well as to computer and computer-controlled machinery. Some of the many ways in which we might employ algorithms and algorithmic reasoning include:

- A recipe and directions for baking double chocolate fudge brownies
- A procedure to taking a patient's blood pressure or performing open heart surgery
- A new app for the latest hand-held phone
- A pilot's flight checklist
- A manual for replacing the transmission in an automobile
- Directions on how to open a savings account for a new bank customer
- A computer program to solve for the roots of a quadratic equation or a system of equations with thousands of equations and variables
- A flight manual for landing an airline jet
- A process for writing a life insurance policy
- A code for building the foundation and structure for a new office building

Common to all of these applications of algorithms is the ability to breakdown the solving of a larger problem or achieving some desired goal into an ordered set of executable steps[1]. Importantly these steps need to be unambiguous and free of omissions and contradiction and will together result in the accomplishment of the objective. While there is not an agreed upon definition of the term, *algorithm*, we will use the following within the context of this document:

The term, "algorithm" is generally attributed to Abū Abdallāh Muḥammad ibn Mūsā al-Khwārizmī who was a Persian astronomer and mathematician and traces back to a treatise he wrote in 825 AD, "On Calculation with Hindu Numerals".

Figure 1-4 - A stamp issued September 6, 1983 in the Soviet Union, commemorating al-Khwārizmī's (approximate) 1200th birthday (Wikipedia - Stamp of al-Khwarizmi)

> **An algorithm is an ordered set of executable steps that are unambiguous and free of omissions and contradictions that will result in the accomplishment of an objective.**

Key parts of this definition include that the steps are ordered and must be able to be directly accomplished (executable). Furthermore, the steps must be free of the possibility of misinterpretation (unambiguous) and that they must not have missing parts (omissions) or cases where conflicting direction is provided (contradictions). Finally, the steps taken as a whole must result in their stated purpose.

Algorithmic reasoning then becomes the ability to effectively develop algorithms for achieving a desired goal and many processes and models exist to help us do so. A few you may have heard of include the Scientific Method, the Engineering Method, the Design Process, the Decision Making Process, and Polya's Problem Solving Technique.

In this text, we use a more general problem solving approach called **UDIT** and pronounced "**U Did IT**".

---

[1] Note that algorithms are typically considered computational processes involving mathematical computations; however, we are broadening the context to a wider range of processes based upon the contention that the problem solving skill sets are highly similar across domains and applications.

1. **Understand** the goal to be accomplished
2. **Design** your solution
3. **Implement** your solution
4. **Test** your solution

Skills with algorithmic reasoning are obviously critical to computer programming as the steps of the algorithm become instructions that are executed by the computer. However, as mentioned early, algorithmic reasoning skills transcend various disciplines and span a wide scope of human endeavors. Yet, most critical to widespread benefit is that the resulting algorithm can be communicated for future reference and for use by others. Think of the role of a manager, team leader, or coach who must orchestrate the efforts of those assigned to them in order to accomplish the group's goal. Not only must they design the process(es) necessary to achieve the objective, but they must also effectively communicate them so that everyone involved will know what they must do to fulfill their part of the effort.

Communicating Algorithms

Algorithms can be communicated in many ways. Perhaps the most simple and natural manner would be via a textual narrative or simple paragraph explaining what needs to be done. The problem with this approach is that it lacks structure and makes it difficult to refer to specific steps. This approach is also prone to ambiguity, omissions, and contradictions.

An obvious improvement upon the narrative form is to create a series of short and concise bullets or a checklist. For instances where the flow through the steps is sequential, this approach works exceedingly well. However, even the bullet format becomes somewhat cumbersome when selection and / or repetition are involved. For example, baking brownies at higher altitudes requires modifications to the process such as lowering temperature and adding flour so alternative steps would be needed based upon the altitude. Furthermore, one might need to repeatedly test the brownies with a toothpick to determine if they are done. The inclusion of selection decisions and repetition can easily introduce confounding levels of complexity to a bullet-oriented checklist form for an algorithm.

This leads us to perhaps the most flexible form of communicating algorithms, the 'flowchart'. The flowchart is a graphical and visual tool where steps and decisions are represented by symbols and arrows designate the flow from one symbol to the next. Flowcharts leverage the visual reasoning skills. These skills are quite natural for most people and, when properly constructed, result in very simple and elegant representations of algorithms.

The "when properly constructed" phrase is a bit ominous. What does it mean to be "properly constructed"? Well, this was a huge problem until the early 1970s, when the Dutch computer scientist, Edsger W. Dijkstra, developed the theory and practice of "structured programming" (Dijkstra, 1970) (Dahl, 1972). The essence of Structured Programming lies in the mathematically proven fact that one only needs three types of control structures (sequence, selection, and iteration) to build an algorithm (program) to solve any problem. Each such construct needs only a single entry and single exit point

Figure 1-5 - Edsger W. Dijkstra (1930-2002)

3

and they can be nested inside of each other to build more complex logic. The structure and discipline that arose from this monumental break-through brought order to the chaos that plagued early computer programs which used an unstructured GOTO construct to jump all around in the code making many programs nearly impossible to understand and maintain.

We have made our way to the 'Structured Flowchart'[2] as our tool of choice for representing algorithms. Now let us learn what these structured flowcharts look like. As mentioned before, flowcharts have symbols (representing steps to be executed) and arrows (to guide us from one symbol to the next). The symbols consist of:

- a rectangle for doing a calculation and storing the result in a variable (a variable is a named location for information can be stored and later referenced),
- a diamond for testing a condition (asking a question) and then directing execution one of two ways based upon the answer,
- a circle for bringing multiple arrows back to the same place or indicating the start or stop points of the algorithm,
- a parallelogram for getting information (input) or reporting results (output),
- a rectangle with an arrow for executing some separate named set of steps (these can be processes that are predefined for us like drawing a circle or separate processes that we make up ourselves to manage complexity or be able to do the same thing over and over again).

To illustrate some of these symbols, the flowchart in Figure 1-6 below provides an algorithm for calculating the area of a circle based upon its radius. Captions in the little bubbles explain what each step is doing.

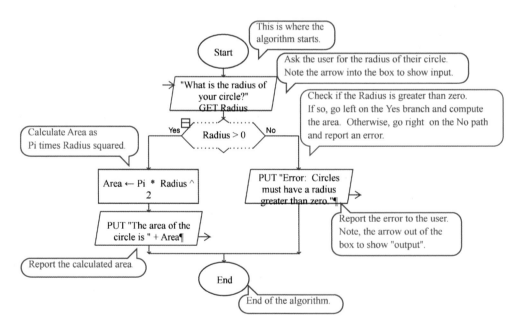

Figure 1-6: Sample RAPTOR Flowchart

---

[2] A Structured Flowchart is a flowchart that complies with the provisions of Structured Programming using only three types of control structures (sequence, selection, and iteration) with single entry and exit points and the ability to nest these structures within each other.

The algorithm begins at the Start circle and then follows the arrow to the next symbol which gets the radius from the user. Following the next arrow brings us to a diamond (somewhat elongated to hold the text, "Radius > 0"). This tests if the value entered in for the Radius is great than zero. If so, we follow the Yes arrow to the left; otherwise we follow the No arrow to the right. On the left side, the area of the circle is calculated and stored in the variable Area and then reported to the user in the next symbol. On the right side, an error message is reported. Both sides then join back together for the single exit point.

Now that you have a basic feel for how these flowcharts work, try to follow through the flowchart in Figure 1-7 below which implements the Hi-Low game. In this game, a random number between 1 and 100 is generated and the user makes guesses as to what the number is. If they guess incorrectly, the algorithm will tell them if they are too high or too low so they can refine their guess for the next turn.

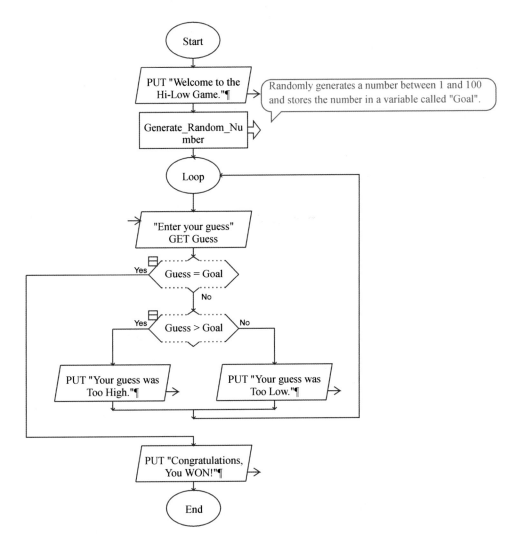

Figure 1-7: Flowchart for the Hi-Low Game

The Hi-Low game algorithm is nice in that it uses all of the flowchart features we have introduced. The Generate_Random_Number rectangle with the large arrow actually runs some separate code which generates a random number between 1 and 100 and places it in a variable called Goal. By making this code separate and giving it a name that corresponds to what it does, we were able to hide (abstract away) the complexity of that process. Doing so is a powerful technique which is appropriately named 'process abstraction' and will be discussed in a later chapter.

The other new construct is the loop. This loop executes once for each turn the user takes. This construct starts at the circle labeled "Loop". This is the point where the arrow from repeating the loop joins up with the arrow that originally brought us into the loop. The exit of the loop construct occurs with the decision based upon "Guess = Goal" which is true (and exits the loop) when the user correctly guesses the random number. Within the loop, the algorithm asks for the next guess, checks if it is correct (and exits if this occurs), and if the guess is incorrect, it continues through the loop making a decision as to whether the guess was high or low and reports the corresponding message before going back up to exit the loop again.

While not a long algorithm, the Hi-Low game algorithm does have a lot going on. Please take some time to trace through it in detail so you feel comfortable with what it is doing. Being able to 'read and understand' an algorithm is a huge initial step leading to algorithmic reasoning; but the exciting and challenging part is actually developing algorithms. Let us talk just a bit about how this can be accomplished.

Constructing Algorithms

The very first and most fundamental step in constructing algorithms is to fully **understand** the objective of the algorithm. This process will likely start with either a narrative or spoken description of the objective. As discussed, these can be an error-prone and inefficient means to describe what is needed for an algorithm, so we'll next break them out into bullets, identifying requirements that need to be satisfied. We'll take care at this point to think about other things that might need to be done but were not explicitly mentioned in the description of the problem. We may also want to create a storyboard sketch describing what our program needs to do and even conduct some analysis of the requirements to ensure that everything is covered and that there are not any conflicting requirements.

With the resulting understanding of the problem, we can create a **design** which involves creating a list of tasks to accomplish, breaking down tasks to smaller tasks as needed, and integrating those tasks with the appropriate control logic (sequence, selection, and iteration) to detail how our program (flowchart) will be built.

The third step is to use our design to actually **implement** the flowchart in RAPTOR. With this we are diving into the details of translating the design into specific programming constructs so that we meet our requirements. Decades of doing this have shown us that it is best to follow Mom's advice and take "one small bite at a time" when doing this. So we break the implement step into small pieces and couple it with the fourth step of test.

In the **test** step, we look through our flowchart and run through it in our mind, as if we were the computer executing it, to make sure that it does everything we need it to. This is called 'desk-checking' and it is very useful as we can think about all the things that could possibly go wrong and make sure that we account for them. Then we run our program (flowchart) with a variety of input to check that it is doing everything the way we want. By coupling implement and test in small steps, we can find and fix problems more easily as most problems that we might find are in the small portion that we just implemented and thus easy to locate and resolve. In this way, we iterate through the construction of our program (flowchart) until we have created a full working version.

The iteration approach is also very useful in that we sometimes find situations that we had not previously considered which need to be addressed by our program or come up with a better way of doing things. When these occur, we way go back to the design or even the understand steps and iterate back through the process. This happens so often that we even have a name for development methods designed to respond to it. We call these "agile methods" and most successful contemporary software is developed in this manner.

So to summarize our problem solving strategy (software development process), we have the outline below:

1. Understand the goal to be accomplished.
   o Carefully review and understand the description and requirements of the problem.
   o Ask any clarifying questions.
   o Maybe make a storyboard to describe what the program must do.
   o Analyze our requirements so that we have covered everything and do not have conflicting requirements.
2. Design your solution.
   o Make a list of tasks that need to be done achieve your goal.
   o Break complex tasks down into smaller sub-tasks.
   o Combine appropriate sequential, conditional, and iterative control logic.
3. Implement your solution.
   o Take small parts of your design and implement them using the programming language (i.e. RAPTOR).
   o Test (next step) that just implemented part of your solution before implementing the next part.
4. Test your solution.
   o Analyze the steps to ensure they will handle all possible cases.
   o Run your program (flowchart) using a variety of inputs to make sure it does what you want.
   o Iterate back to update your implementation, design, or even understanding as needed.

Let us try constructing the two algorithms we have seen thus far.

1. Calculate the area of a circle

With simple problem statements like this, the narrative description gives us exactly what our goal is – find the area of a circle (Understand). As we think about the problem more, we can design our solution by identifying a list of tasks to accomplish. For an algorithm to find the area of a circle, we'll need to do the following:

- Obtain the radius of the circle from the user
- Check that the radius is greater than zero and provide an error message if it is not
- Calculate the area as Pi times the radius squared
- Report the area to the user

The Area of a Circle algorithm is an example of a simple Input-Process-Output algorithm – input the radius, process to compute the area, and output the area. The second sub-task of checking whether the radius is positive may not have been given to us in the original description, but it illustrates the idea of making our algorithm robust and able to nicely handle whatever the user throws at it.

The initial cut at the Area of a Circle algorithm asks the user for radius and then checks that the entered value was positive. This is a sequence of two steps, where the second step is a Selection statement, as shown implemented in Figure 1-8.

Next, we think about what to do in each of the two cases. If the Radius is greater than zero, we'll calculate the Area and then report it to the user (a sequence of two steps nested within the Yes branch of the selection.) For the No side, we'll just report the error (a sequence of one step). This results in our complete algorithm, as shown in Figure 1-9.

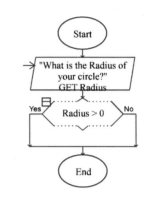

Figure 1-8: Initial Iteration of the Flowchart Implementation

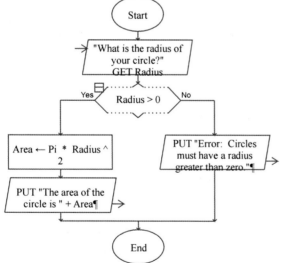

Figure 1-9: Complete Area of a Circle Flowchart

We would then review and test the algorithm with some sample input values for Radius like 1, 10, and -1. The Radius of 1 should produce an output of "The area of the circle is 3.1416". The Radius of 10 should result in "The area of the circle is 314.1593". And finally, the Radius of -1 would give "Error: Circles must have a radius greater than zero."

The key idea is simply to make a list of what needs to be done and work our way through the process of putting the steps in the correct order and within the appropriate control structures. Now let's give it a try on the Hi-Low game.

8

2. Play the Hi-Low Game

First, we need to read through the description of the game provided in Communicating Algorithms and make sure we fully understand the rules and requirements, asking any clarifying questions we may have (i.e. the Understand step). Once we have read through and understand the description, we realize that we will begin the Design step and develop a list of tasks to accomplish (as listed below):

- Welcome the player to the game
- Generate a goal number for the player to guess
- Repeatedly have the player make guesses until they guess the number
- If they guess too high or too low, let them know
- When they guess correctly, let them know that they have won

Following the idea of Build-a-Little, Test-a-Little, we would then start putting our Design List of Tasks into a nice structured flowchart. An initial cut might look something like the flowchart in Figure 1-10 where we address the first two steps and set up a loop for repeating the player's turns. Generating a random number is something that we do not quite know how to do yet and it might be a bit complex so we make that a separate sub-chart and deal with it as a distinct problem.

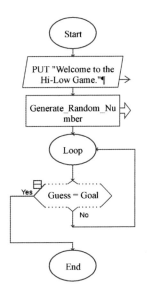

Figure 1-10: Initial Cut at the Hi-Low Game Algorithm Implementation

Next, we would think about what happens within a player turn and add an input construct to get the player's guess. We could also report a victory message when we exit the loop, as shown in Figure 1-11.

9

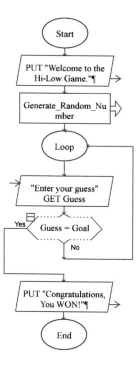

Figure 1-11: Second Implementation Iteration for the Hi-Low Game Algorithm

Finally, we would consider what needs to happen when the player does not guess correctly. This would involve a selection that would occur after we check the user's guess, as shown in Figure 1-12. Why is it important that this selection occurs after the check for a correct guess[3]?

With the algorithm constructed, we would then test it (i.e. the Test step). To do this we would walk through the flowchart and track the values in the variables. We can assume that Goal would take on some appropriate value like 37. (Note, we can see the value in the Goal variable via RAPTOR's Debug window in the lower right part of the RAPTOR programming environment which will make this testing easy). Then we could assume the player guess something high like 50 (which would go into the Guess variable). The result would be that the "Your guess was Too High" message is displayed. We would then guess too low like 25 and see that the "Your guess was Too Low" message appropriately gets displayed. Finally, we would assume a guess of 37 to see that the loop exits and the "Congratulations, You WON!" message is presented.

---

[3] If we did the "Guess > Goal" selection before the "Guess = Goal" exit check, a correct answer would always take the No branch as 'equals to' is part of 'not greater than'.

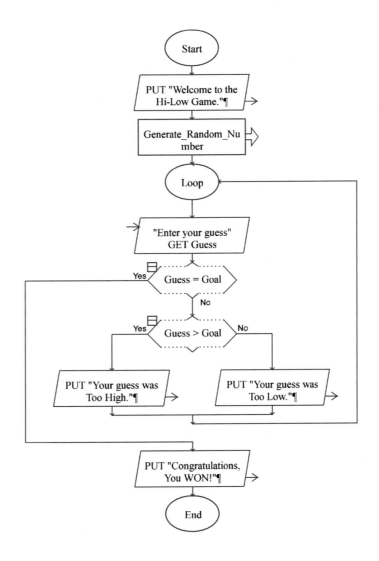

Figure 1-2: Final Hi-Low Game Algorithm

So to summarize, with the Understand step, we carefully read and studied the description of the Hi-Low game asking questions to ensure that our understanding was correct. The for the Design step we made a list of tasks that needed to be done and then put the steps in the correct order and the appropriate control structures. For the Implementation step, we built up our Hi-Low game algorithm in three manageable iterations checking each one as we went. For the final Test step, we ran the Hi-Low game algorithm with a variety of inputs making sure each path through the flowchart was working correctly.

In general, the construction of algorithms is non-trivial to say the least. Furthermore, it is a skill that this text is designed to help you develop. We'll need to work our way through a few more chapters before we are ready to build algorithms like the Hi-Low game for ourselves (so don't let this algorithm intimidate you at this point). The good news is that as our algorithmic reasoning skills develop, so does our ability to solve more complex problems, build interesting systems, and communicate our algorithms to others (including to computers as programs).

Exercises

1. Write an algorithm that accepts the height and width of a rectangle and calculates and reports the length of its perimeter and its area.

2. Write an algorithm that accepts the radius and height of a cylinder and then calculates and reports the volume of the cylinder.

3. Write an algorithm to bake chocolate chip cookies.

4. Write an algorithm to get dressed in the morning. You might add in consideration of what the day's activities entail.

5. Write an algorithm for determining who wins a game of Rock-Paper-Scissors.

6. Write an algorithm for playing Tic-Tac-Toe.

7. Write an algorithm for keeping track of the score for a game of bowling.

8. What is the problem with the following algorithm: Lather, Rinse, Repeat?

9. How would you extend the Hi-Low game algorithm to count the number tries that the player takes to guess the number? How would you change the algorithm so that the player only has seven tries to guess the answer?

10. Write an algorithm that calculates the roots of a quadratic equation in the form:

$$a x^2 + b x + c = 0$$

    Recall that the quadratic formal is:

$$x = \frac{-b \pm \sqrt{b^2 - 4 a c}}{2 a}$$

    Note that if the expression $b^2 - 4 a c$ is positive, there are two real roots. If it is zero, there is one repeated root. If it is negative, there are two complex conjugate roots. You may just want to consider the two real root case.

11. Think of some process that you are familiar with and write an algorithm for accomplishing it using a structured flowchart.

2. Basic Sequential Algorithms: An Introduction to RAPTOR with Input-Process-Output Algorithms

Thus far we have learned that algorithmic reasoning is a powerful problem solving technique applicable across a wide variety of purposes. We have also learned that flowcharts are a very precise and efficient means to build and represent algorithms. Starting in this chapter, we will start creating and executing flowcharts using the RAPTOR visual programming environment. These flowcharts will solve a wide variety of problems and allow us to build interesting graphical animations and computer games.

As we create our RAPTOR flowcharts, we will be developing and practicing our algorithmic reasoning skills as well as learning about the concepts and techniques used to create computer software. Professor Martin Carlisle specifically designed RAPTOR to help us achieve these goals in an easy and efficient manner leveraging our abilities for visual understanding and minimizing the need to memorize a large set of programming rules.

A Quick Tour of RAPTOR

Before we start creating RAPTOR algorithms, let us familiarize ourselves with the key components of RAPTOR. The color-coded diagram (Figure 2-1) below identifies the five primary components of the RAPTOR environment.

- The Menu and Tool Bar area provides access to commands and features of RAPTOR, such as the ability to save and run our flowcharts.
- The Workspace contains the flowcharts that we develop and run.
- The Symbol Palette provides a means for us to put symbols into our flowcharts.
- The Watch Window enables us to see the value in each of our variables.
- The Master Console displays the output of our algorithms and can also show a log of our activities while creating the flowchart.

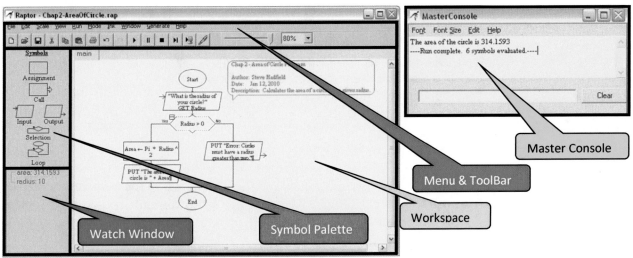

Figure 2-1: RAPTOR Programming Environment

Creating Algorithms in RAPTOR

We can create our flowchart algorithms in RAPTOR using any of three mechanisms. First, we can click and drag symbols from the Symbol Palette to the flowchart in the Workspace. Second, we can right-click on an arrow in the flowchart and then insert symbols from the menu that appears. Finally, we can select a symbol from the Symbol Palette and then click on the flowchart arrows where we would like to insert that symbol.

Once we have added a symbol to our flowchart, we can either double-click on it or right-click and select Edit to specify the details for that symbol. Each of the symbols have their own set of details to specify. We will go through three of them in this chapter: Assignment, Input, and Output. The remaining three, Call, Selection, and Loop, will be addressed later.

When starting a new flowchart in RAPTOR, we begin with two special symbols – the Start circle and the End circle which are connected by an arrow, see Figure 2-2. We build our flowcharts between this single entry point (Start circle) and the single exit point (Exit circle).

Figure 2-2: Start of a New Flowchart

We can then add symbols using a drop-and-drag from the Symbol Palette, right-click on an arrow, or select from the Symbol Palette with a left-click to add.

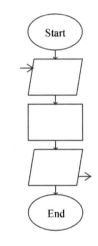

After adding an Input, an Assignment, and an Output symbol, our flowchart would look like the one in Figure 2-3. This input-process-output (IPO) format is a common and simple form of algorithms where the input obtains information from the user, the process (assignment) does some calculation on that input, and the output reports the results back to the user.

Note that the Input symbol has an arrow coming into it from the left and the output symbol has an arrow going out of it to the right to help us distinguish between these two similar operations.

Figure 2-3: Input-Process-Output Flowchart

Next we will learn how to specify the details for each of these symbols. By doing so we make each one an executable step of our algorithm. However, before we do that, we need to understand the concept of a variable.

Variables

A **variable** is a named location where we can store values and then later look up those values. Variables have both a **name** which we use to reference it and a **value** which is the contents held in the variable. Variables in RAPTOR may hold either numbers (such as 5 or 3.141593) or strings (which are groups of characters such as "Sally" or "The dog barked at the cat.").

The name of the variable is very important as it will help us keep track of the information being processed by our algorithm. We want to name each variable so the name accurately and explicitly describes the information that it is holding, sometimes using several words. However we have to be careful as our variable names may not include spaces because it is impossible to distinguish between a two-word name for a single variable versus two distinct variables. Therefore, when we use multiple words for a variable name, we either put an underscore (_) between them or simply squash them together, usually capitalizing the first letter of the second and later words to help call them out. Note we cannot start variable names with digits or include special characters as these make it difficult to distinguish variables from numbers and other operations in RAPTOR. The table 2-1 provides some examples of good, bad, and illegal variable names.

Table 2-1: Examples of Good, Bad, and Illegal Variable Names

Good variable names	Poor variable names		Illegal variable names	
tax_rate	a	(not descriptive)	4sale	(does not start with a letter)
salesTax	milesperhour	(add underscores)	sales tax	(includes a space)
distance_in_miles	my4to	(not descriptive)	sales$	(includes invalid character)
mpg				

Importantly, variables in RAPTOR can also hold strings of characters such as "Sally" or "Welcome to my program". Strings significantly expand the capabilities of RAPTOR and allow us to easily handle text-based information.

Input Symbol

A common way to place a value into a variable is with an Input symbol. When you open up the details for an Input symbol (by either a double-click or right-click and select Edit), the Enter Input dialog box in Figure 2-4 is displayed, allowing us to specify two parameters. The first is a prompt which is simply text that asks the user to provide the specific input. The second parameter is the name of the variable where the entered value will be stored.

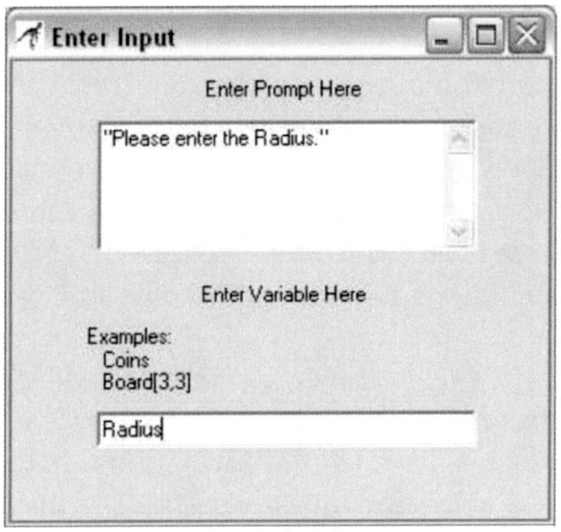

The Input dialog box in Figure 2-5 corresponds to the Input symbol below. When this symbol is executed, the Input dialog box to the right of the symbol appears. Whatever value is typed into the text box will be put into the variable, Radius, when the OK button is clicked.

Figure 2-4: Input Symbol Dialog Box

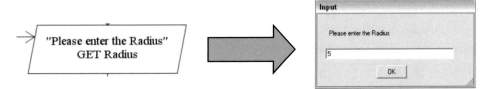

Figure 2-5: Input Symbol with Corresponding Input Dialog Box

15

For the Prompt, any text in quotes will be displayed directly as-is for the user. We could also include the name of a variable (without quotes) in which case the value in that variable would be displayed. Furthermore, we could combine quoted text with variables by putting a plus sign (+) between them to create prompts that provide additional information. An example might be a prompt such as in Figure 2-6.

"Hello " + User_Name + ", please enter value #" + Current_Number

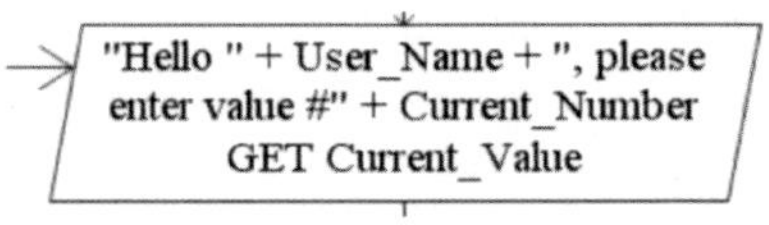

Figure 2-6: Prompt with Quoted Text and Variables

Here, both User_Name and Current_Number are variables and the rest is quoted text. If User_Name contained the string, "Sally" and Current_Number contained the numeric value of 3, the resulting prompt would read as shown in Figure 2-7.

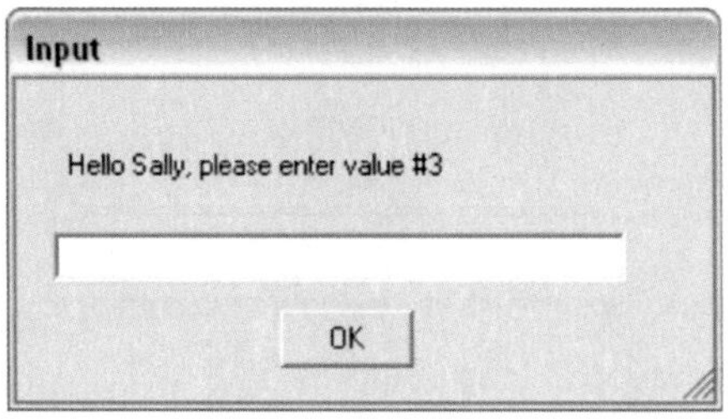

Figure 2-7: Input Box with Prompt Using Quoted Text and Variables

Assignment Symbol

We can also put values into variables with the Assignment symbol. This can be done either directly by giving the exact value that we want in the variable or by evaluating some expression whose results will be placed into the variable. The expression evaluation approach provides a very powerful calculation tool as we can do both arithmetic operations as well as call functions. Function calls allow even more advanced computations such as square roots and logarithms.

When we open the Enter Statement dialog box for an Assignment symbol, the form to specify its two parameters is displayed, see Figure 2-8. The first parameter, next to the 'Set' prompt, is the name of the variable in which we are going to store a value or the results of a calculation. The second parameter, by the 'to' prompt, is the number, string, or expression that will be evaluated to determine the value to assign to the variable. In this case, the variable Area will be assigned the value that results from multiplying Pi (3.141593…) by the value of Radius squared. Here 'Pi' is a named constant defined with the correct value by RAPTOR. Importantly, it is the 'to' part that is evaluated first and the results placed into the variable in the 'Set' part. The resulting Assignment symbol is shown in Figure 2-9.

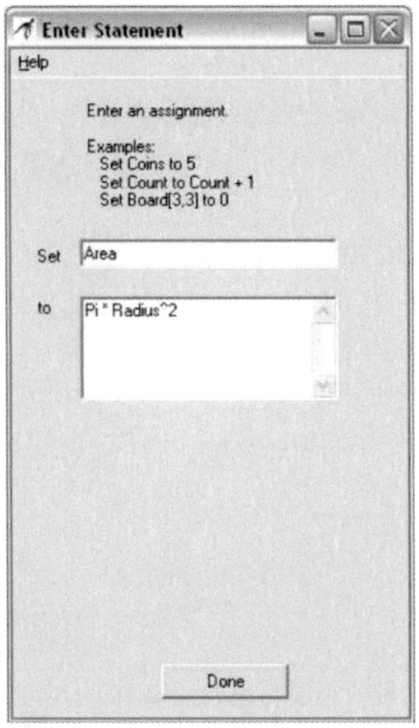

Figure 2-8: Enter Statement Dialog Box

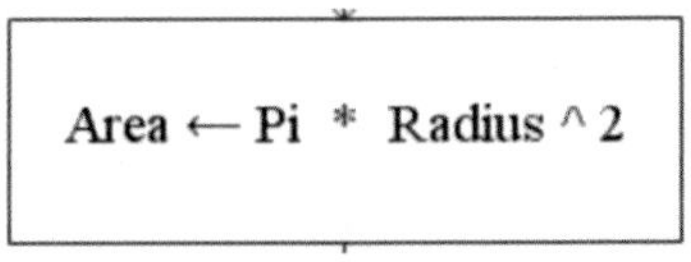

$$\boxed{\text{Area} \leftarrow \text{Pi} \; * \; \text{Radius} \; ^\wedge \, 2}$$

Figure 2-9: Resulting Assignment Symbol

Within RAPTOR, you have all of the standard arithmetic operations such as + (addition), - (subtraction), * (multiplication), / (division), and ^ (or **) for exponentiation. RAPTOR also has the REM and MOD functions for remainder and modulus, respectively.

Within a RAPTOR expression, the normal order of operation rules apply. These rules are:

1. Evaluate all functions
2. Evaluate sub-expressions in parentheses (innermost first)
3. Evaluate unary minus (like -5)
4. Evaluate exponentiation
5. Evaluate multiplication and division (left to right)
6. Evaluate addition and subtraction (left to right)

The expression **Pi * Radius^2** actually gets evaluated as **Pi * (Radius^2)**. Of course, the safe approach is to always fully specify your order of operations using parentheses to avoid problems that can be very difficult to find.

Importantly, we need to understand that variables will take on different values at different times. In the example in Figure 2-10, the variables Height and Width are assigned the values 3 and 4, respectively. Then the variable Rectangle_Area is assigned the value of 12 which is obtained by multiplying Width times Height. Then the Width variable is assigned a new value of 5. Finally, the Rectangle_Area value is assigned a new value of 15 by multiplying Width (with its new value of 5) time Height (with its unchanged value of 3).

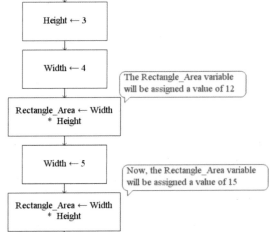

Figure 2-10: Example of Multiple Assignment Statements in Sequence

Expressions in RAPTOR can also include a wide variety of mathematical functions which may take in values and always return results. Table 2-2 on the next page presents the functions that are available in RAPTOR.

Table 2-2: Functions Available in RAPTOR

Function	Description	Example
rem mod	remainder (what is left over) when the right operand divides the left operand	10 rem 3 is 1 10 mod 4 is 2
sqrt	square root	sqrt(4) is 2
log	natural logarithm (base e)	log(e) is 1
abs	absolute value	abs(-9) is 9
ceiling	rounds up to a whole number	ceiling(3.14159) is 4
floor	rounds down to a whole number	floor(9.82) is 9
sin	trig sin(angle_in_radians)	sin(pi/6) is 0.5
cos	trig cos(angle_in_radians)	cos(pi/3) is 0.5
tan	trig tan(angle_in_radians)	tan(pi/4) is 1.0
cot	trig cotangent(angle_in_radians)	cot(pi/4) is 1
arcsin	trig $\sin^{-1}$(expression), returns radians	arcsin(0.5) is pi/6
arcos	trig $\cos^{-1}$(expression), returns radians	arccos(0.5) is pi/3
arctan	trig $\tan^{-1}$(y,x), returns radians	arctan(10,3) is 1.2793
arccot	trig $\cot^{-1}$(x,y), returns radians	arccot(10,3) is 0.29145
random	generates a random value in the range [0.0, 1.0)	random * 100 is some value between 0 and 99.9999

Output Symbol

The Output symbol allows us to report the results of our calculations to the Master Console window. This symbol has one primary parameter which is the expression to be evaluated and then displayed. This expression could be as simple as a single variable (whose value will be displayed) or some quoted text that will be displayed exactly as presented. Alternatively, the expression could be like any of the expressions that we could create for the Assignment symbol. This flexibility allows us to do calculations in the Output symbol directly, but the results of expressions in the Output symbol are not stored in a variable for later use. Figure 2-11 provides an example of the Enter Output dialog box.

At the bottom of the dialog for the Output symbol is an "End current line" check box. If checked, this will cause any subsequent output to be on the next line in the Master Console. If unchecked, any subsequent output would be immediately following this current output. The Output symbol in Figure 2-12 corresponds to the Output dialog box to the right. The paragraph symbol (¶) is present because the

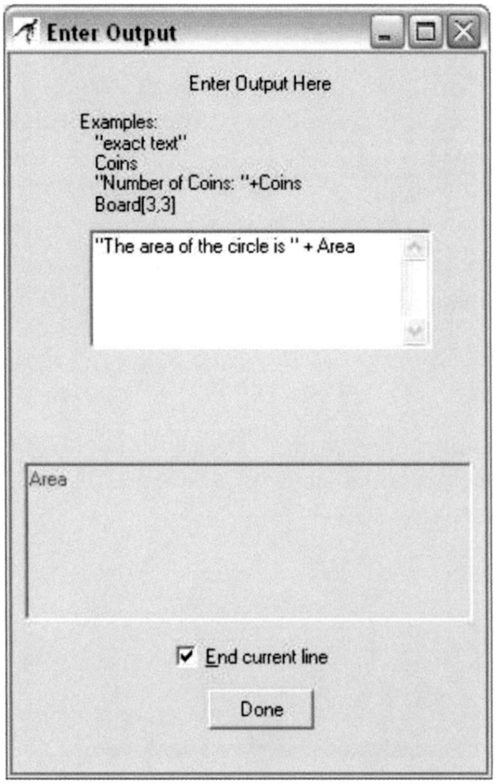

Figure 2-11: Enter Output Dialog Box

"End current line" was checked and will cause any subsequent output to occur on a separate line.

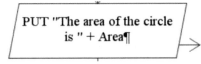

Figure 2-12: Output Symbol Example

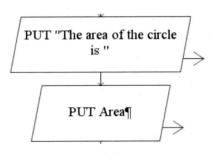

Alternatively, we could have used two Output symbols; one for the text, "The area of the circle is ", and a separate one for the value of the Area variable (as shown in Figure 2-13). We would not check "End current line" for the first one which would put both outputs on the same line.

Figure 2-13: Two Symbol Output Sequence

An Example Input-Process-Output (IPO) Algorithm

To bring what we have learned in this chapter together and relate it to the algorithmic reasoning approach to problem solving from the previous chapter, we will create an algorithm (as a RAPTOR flowchart) to solve a simple problem. We start off with a narrative description of our problem which is:

Calculate the distance between two points: (x_1, y_1) and (x_2, y_2).

This problem is fairly straight forward, so we can consider our first step, understanding the problem, complete. Our next problem solving activity is to design a solution by breaking it down into a list of tasks. The resulting list of tasks could look something like the following:

- Get the two points from the user
- Calculate the distance between the points
- Report the calculated distance to the user

This is a great start and directly follows our Input-Process-Output (IPO) organization. However, we may need to analyze each step in a bit more detail. Specifically, we have two points to get from the user and each point has two values, X and Y. To calculate the distance, we need to use the Pythagorean Theorem (illustrated in Figure 2-14) which requires we know the difference in X values between the two points as well as the difference in Y values.

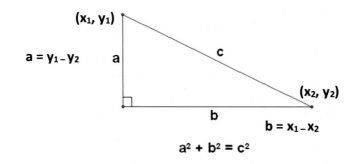

Figure 2-14: Distance between Two Points Using the Pythagorean Theorem

This is getting a bit more complicated so we will take each of the tasks in our original list of tasks and create a list of sub-tasks for each. We now have the multi-level design shown in the bullets below.

- Get the two points from the user
  - Get X value for the first point, x_1
  - Get Y value for the first point, y_1
  - Get X value for the second point, x_2
  - Get Y value for the second point, y_2
- Calculate the distance between the points
  - Calculate the difference in X values between the two points (call this **b**)
  - Calculate the difference in Y values between the two points (call this **a**)
  - Use the Pythagorean Theorem ($c^2 = a^2 + b^2$) to calculate the distance **c** as $\sqrt{a^2 + b^2}$
- Report the calculated distance to the user
  - Describe the results as the distance between the two points: (x_1, y_1) and (x_2, y_2)
  - Report the calculated distance

With this multi-level design, we now have all the pieces that we will need to implement our algorithm as a RAPTOR flowchart as each of the sub-bullets above can be implemented with just one or two symbols. The resulting RAPTOR flowchart is shown in Figure 2-15. We would then test it with some sample inputs to make sure that it is working as intended. Some good sample test cases could be those shown in Table 2-3. Take a close look at each of the pairs of points. What different situations do they test?

Table 2-3: Example Good Test Inputs

Inputs	(0, 0) and (3, 4)	(1, 1) and (4, 5)	(0, -5) and (0, 1)	(1, 3) and (5, 3)	(4, 7) and (4, 7)
Results	5	5	6	4	0

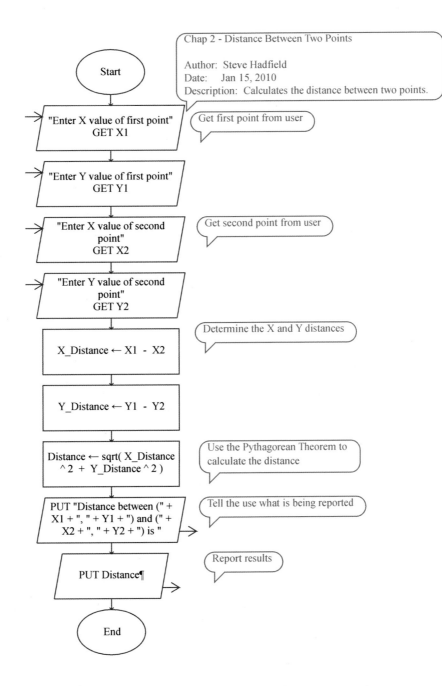

Figure 2-15: Flowchart for Calculating the Distance between Two Points

Hopefully this example has given you a good idea of how we can start with a problem statement, understand what needs to be done, design a solution (in this case using multiple levels), implement the solution, and then test our solution. This distance between two points calculation is important and will be used later when we develop some game algorithms, so it will be worthwhile for you to take a few extra minutes to fully understand it.

Comments

In the RAPTOR flowchart for calculating the distance between two points, we see that there are green captions that describe what is being done at various points in the algorithm. These are called **Comments**, and they are an important tool in communicating what the flowchart is intending to do so others who read it (and ourselves after we come back to it later on) can more easily understand the flowchart. We enter comments by right-clicking on a symbol and selecting **Comment** from the pop-up menu. A dialog box appears and allows us to specify our comments as shown in Figure 2-16.

We should include Comments at least every few symbols to describe what we intend the next few symbols to accomplish. This is especially important when more complicated expressions are involved. We should also have a Comment at the very beginning of our flowchart which identifies the flowchart and provides the name of author, date it was created, and a description of what it does.

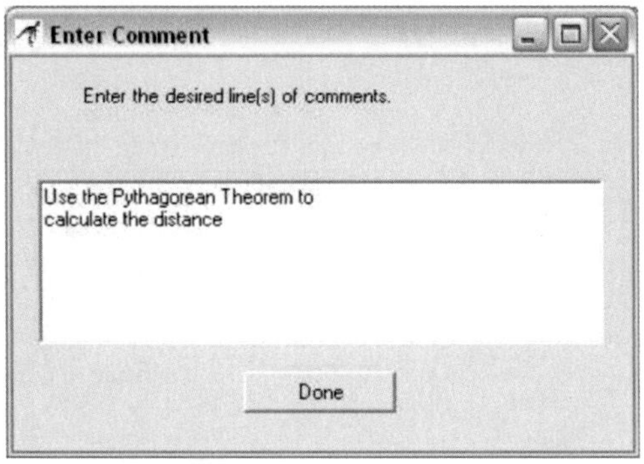

Figure 2-16: Example Enter Comment Dialog Box

Running and Debugging Flowcharts

Before attempting to run or debug a flowchart, one should always save the file first (via either File | Save or the Save button on the tool bar). In fact, RAPTOR will force you to save your problem after the first minute or so of starting to work on it to prevent you from losing your entire program. Furthermore, it will periodically save back-up copies (.bak extension) to help protect you from losing your work. However, it is best to get into the practice of saving your work every few minutes.

To run a RAPTOR flowchart, we have two alternatives. The Execute to Completion button runs the flowchart one symbol after the next automatically. The Slider bar controls how fast RAPTOR goes to the next symbol. All the way to the right is full speed. Moving the slider to the left slows the execution so you can watch the values in variables change as the flowchart executes.

The other way to run the flowchart is one symbol at a time. This is done by clicking the Step to Next Shape button . Running RAPTOR in this way pauses execution and waits for the next click after each symbol is run and provides a wonderful way to check that your flowchart is doing what you intended it to do.

In either mode, the Watch Window will display the name and current value for each of your variables. Variables that have just taken on new values will be shown in Red while the others will be in Black so we can easily see what is changing as we go through the program.

We can also pause or stop the flowchart with the following two buttons: . In addition, we can right-click on any symbol and select Toggle Breakpoint. When the Breakpoint is on, a red circle shows by the symbol and execution of the flowchart will stop at this point so we can check the variables to see what is going on. See Figure 2-17 for an example of a RAPTOR program with a Breakpoint. This can be a tremendous help in locating problems with flowcharts that are not working as intended or in just checking that everything is working as expected.

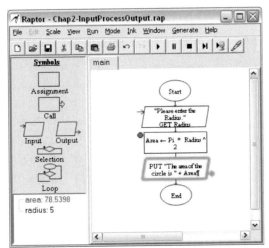

Figure 2-17: RAPTOR Program with a Breakpoint

Of course all of the various modes of running flowcharts in RAPTOR can be used in combination which makes the testing and debugging of RAPTOR flowcharts very easy to accomplish. This will become even more interesting (and complicated) as we learn to do more with RAPTOR. We will revisit this concept in subsequent chapters.

Conclusion

In this chapter we have learned about the RAPTOR programming environment and how we can use it to create and run algorithms represented as flowcharts. This approach makes great use of our visual reasoning abilities while also minimizing the amount of details that we need to know to create running algorithms. RAPTOR provides us an outstanding tool for developing our algorithmic reasoning skills starting with some basic input-process-output (IPO) format algorithms.

Admiral Grace Murray Hopper was one of the first computer programming pioneers and the inventor of the COBOL programming language. She is also credited with coined the term "computer bug".

On the 9th of September, 1947, the Harvard University Mark II Aiken Relay Calculator (a primitive computer) started to experience some problems. Upon investigation, it was found that there was a moth trapped between the points of Relay #70, in Panel F.

The operators removed the moth and affixed it to the log. (See the picture below.) The entry reads: "First actual case of bug being found."

The word went out that they had "debugged" the machine and the term "debugging a computer program" was born.

Although Grace Hopper was always careful to admit that she was not there when it actually happened, but it was one of her favorite stories.

(http://www.jamesshuggins.com/h/tek1/first_computer_bug.htm)

Exercises

1. Write an algorithm that accepts the height and width of a rectangle and calculates and reports the length of its perimeter and its area.

2. Write an algorithm that accepts the radius and height of a cylinder and then calculates and reports the volume of the cylinder.

3. Write an algorithm that accepts the amount of a restaurant bill and a tip (gratuity) percentage and then calculates and reports the tip amount and the total amount with gratuity.

4. Write an algorithm to help you plan for an upcoming car trip. Your algorithm needs to accept the distance to travel (in miles), the miles-per-gallon (MPG) for your car, and the price of a gallon of gas. The algorithm will then calculate and report the total number of gallons of gas that you should expect to use and the total cost of that amount of gas.

5. Write an algorithm that accepts a person's weight and calculates and reports their corresponding weight on other planets. You can do this by multiplying the person's Earth weight by the following constants for each of the planets; Mercury: 0.38, Venus: 0.91, Mars: 0.38, Jupiter: 2.34, Saturn: 1.06, Uranus: 0.92, Neptune: 1.19, and Pluto: 0.06. Reference: https://www.livescience.com/33356-weight-on-planets-mars-moon.html.

6. An earthquake's power is typically measure using the Richter Scale where each successive whole number magnitude is 33 times more powerful. For example, a 7.0 magnitude earthquake is 33 times more powerful than a 6.0 magnitude earthquake. Furthermore, an 8.0 magnitude earthquake is 33 x 33 or 1089 times more powerful than a 6.0 magnitude earthquake. Write an algorithm that accepts the Richter Scale magnitude of a smaller earthquake followed by the magnitude of a larger earthquake and then calculates and reports how much more powerful the larger earthquake is compared to the smaller earthquake. Use the formula: 33^(larger_magnitude – smaller_magnitude). Reference: https://www.livescience.com/31464-earthquake-magnitude-explained.html.

7. **CHALLENGE EXERCISE:** The distance between two points on the surface of the Earth can be calculated based on the Great Circle distance using the Haversine formula. Write an algorithm that accepts two locations expressed as latitudes and longitudes each given in terms of degrees, minutes, seconds, and direction (N, S, E, W). Convert the degrees, minutes, and seconds into a single angle value as follows:

$$angl\_in\_degrees = degrees + \frac{minutes}{60} + \frac{seconds}{3600}$$

Convert each $angle\_in\_degrees$ into radians as follows:

$$angle\_in\_radians = angle\_in\_degrees * \frac{\pi}{180}$$

For West longitudes and South latitudes, make the angles negative.

Calculate the Haversine formula in the following three parts:

$$a = \sin^2\left(\frac{lat2 - lat1}{2}\right) + \left(\cos(lat1) * \cos(lat2) * \sin^2\left(\frac{long2 - long1}{2}\right)\right)$$

$$c = 2 * arctan\left(\sqrt{a}, \sqrt{(1-a)}\right)$$

$$distance = R * c$$

where R is the average radius of the Earth (6,371km or 3959 miles) and the two points on the earth are $(lat1, long1)$ and $(lat2, long2)$ where these latitudes and longitudes have been converted to single values in radians. Reference: https://www.movable-type.co.uk/scripts/latlong.html.

3. Graphics and the Procedure Call: Drawing Pictures and Interacting Using the Mouse

Computer graphics and animations have revolutionized the way human beings interact with computers and have significantly increased our enjoyment of using computers. This chapter introduces the graphics capabilities of RAPTOR so we can use them throughout the remainder of this text to make your experiences with RAPTOR even more enjoyable.

Procedures and Process Abstraction

Within RAPTOR, we create and interact with graphics via a set of built-in **procedures.** A **procedure** is a named process that we can call (via the Call symbol) to have that process done for us. The built-in RAPTOR procedures allow us to do things such as create graphics windows, draw shapes in those windows, display text in the windows, and interact using either the mouse or keyboard. These appear to be complicated operations, but we do not have to worry about that. All we have to do is to call these procedures and they will perform their operations for us. We do not have to know nor care **how** they do this. We just need to know **what** they can do for us. We call this concept **Process Abstraction,** as the details of the processing performed have been abstracted away for us. We need just focus on the high level operation that is provided, such as drawing a rectangle of a specified color at a given location. This leads us to the following two definitions:

> **Procedure – is a named set of instructions that implement some meaningful operation and which we can call to have that operation performed whenever needed.**
>
> **Process Abstraction – is the concept whereby the details of how a procedure accomplishes its operation are hidden. All we need to do is to call the procedure to accomplish its operation.**

Importantly, we always strive to name our procedures to accurately describe the function that they perform such as Open_Graphics_Window, Draw_Box, Draw_Circle, Display_Text, or Get_Mouse_Button.

To have a procedure perform its operation, we simply use a Call symbol within the RAPTOR Flowchart. An Enter Call dialog box displays a single text box in which the procedure name (possibly with parameters) can be entered. In Figure 3-1, the Enter Call dialog box has a call to the built-in RAPTOR procedure Draw_Box. To the right is the resulting RAPTOR flowchart symbol that is produced.

This Draw_Box call includes not only the name of the procedure being called but also six parameters; which in this case happen to be the (X, Y) position of the one corner of the box, the (X, Y) position of the opposite corner, the color of the box, and an indication to fill the box with that color (as opposed to just making the boundary of the box that color). Parameters such as these are used to tailor the procedure's operation.

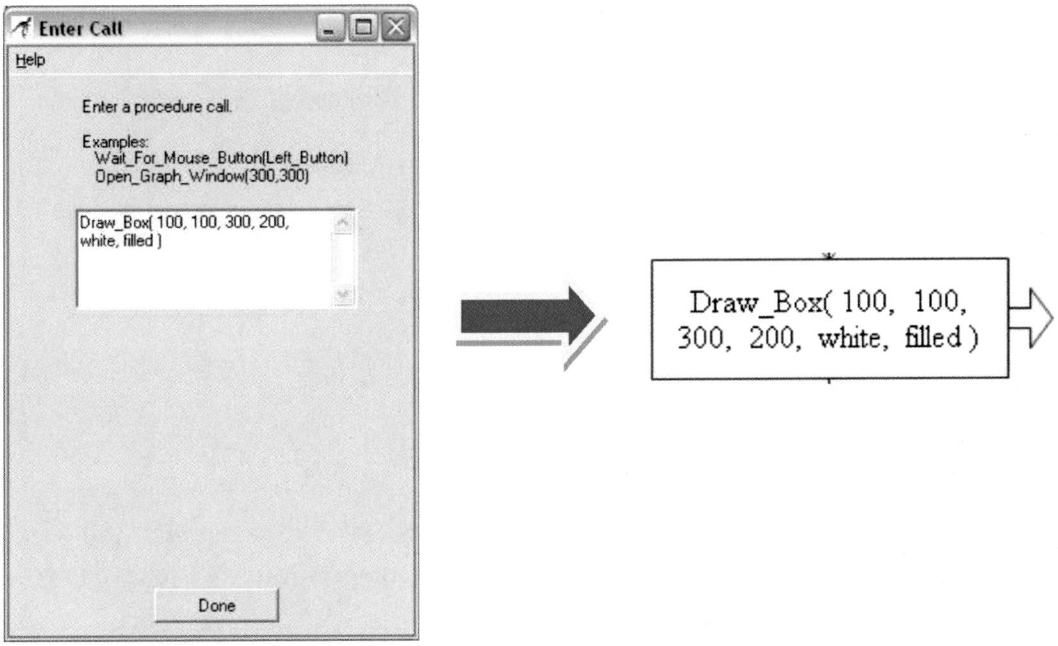

Figure 3-1: Enter Call Dialog Box with Resulting Call Symbol

Later on we will be creating our own procedures using subcharts, but for now, we only need to use those procedures already defined for us.

Introduction to Graphics in RAPTOR

Now that we have a notion of procedures and process abstraction, we are ready to get started with graphics. All graphics in RAPTOR are done in the **Graphics Window,** which is shown in Figure 3-2.

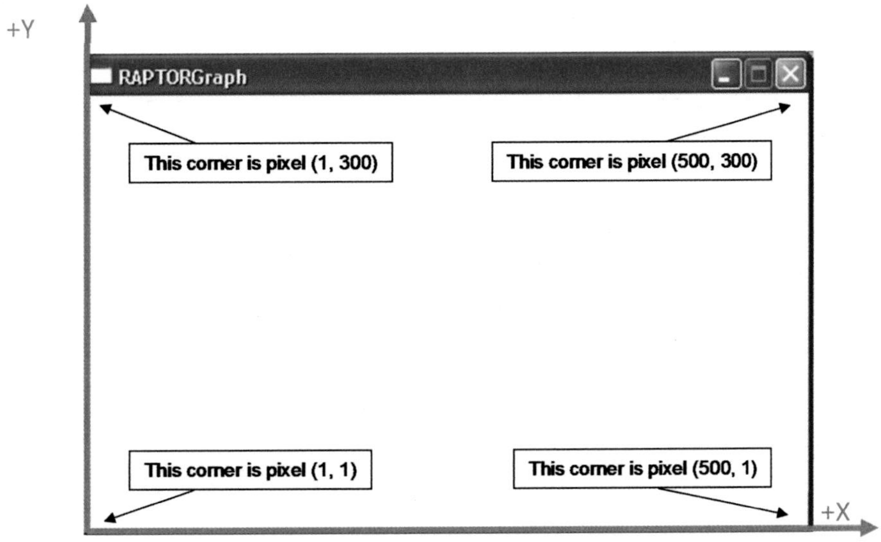

Figure 3-2: RAPTOR Graphics Window

27

The graphics window is laid out as a two dimensional grid with an X and Y coordinate system. We use these coordinates to draw shapes on the graphics window.

For our first RAPTOR flowchart using graphics, we will do the following:

- Open a graphics window that is 400 pixels wide and 300 pixels high.
- Set the title bar of the graphics window to "RAPTOR – Graphics Introduction – Left click to exit".
- Clear the graphics window setting the background color to light blue.
- Draw a white box in the middle of the graphics window using the coordinate system above.
- Set the text font size to 30 points.
- Display the word, "RAPTOR", in the middle of the white box.
- Wait for the user to left click the mouse.
- Close the graphics window.

The RAPTOR flowchart to accomplish this is shown in Figure 3-3 together with the resulting graphics window in Figure 3-4. **Note, the graphics window must be open before we can do any graphics calls.**

With this program (and indeed most graphics programs), we explicitly wait for the user to indicate they are done, in this case via a left mouse click, before closing the graphics window. If we had not done this, the graphics would have flashed up and then quickly closed without the user being able to see what we created. We also need to take care to always close the graphics window before exiting the program; otherwise the window will remain displayed.

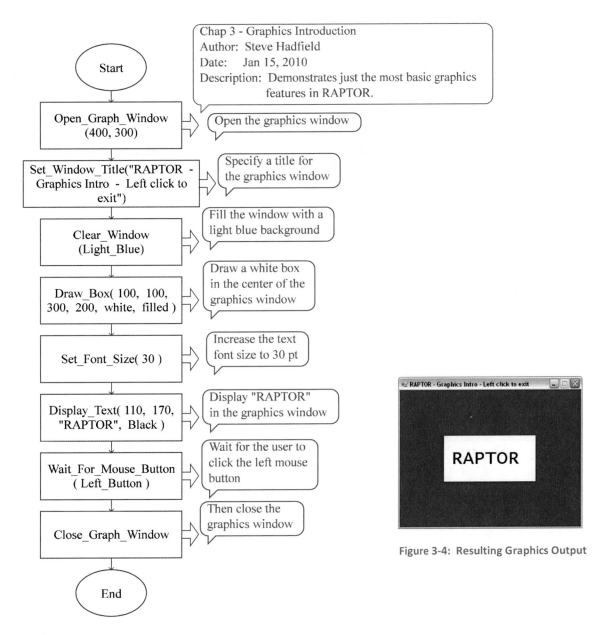

Figure 3-4: Resulting Graphics Output

Figure 3-3: A First RAPTOR Graphics Program

Drawing Objects in RAPTORGraph

RAPTOR offers a full set of basic drawing routines which allow us to create many different graphical displays. The table below identifies the drawing procedures available in RAPTOR. Additional details and examples are readily available in the RAPTOR help system. Notice that in most of these you first provide the location, possibly the size, followed by the color, and then an indication of whether or not the shape is to be filled with the color or just the border is to be drawn in that color (Unfilled).

29

Shape	Procedure Call With Description
line	`Draw_Line(X1, Y1, X2, Y2, Color)` Draws a straight line between (X1,Y1) and (X2,Y2) of the specified color.
rectangle	`Draw_Box(X1, Y1, X2, Y2, Color, Filled/Unfilled)` Draws a rectangle by specifying any corner of the box, (X1,Y1) and the opposite corner, (X2,Y2).
circle	`Draw_Circle(X, Y, Radius, Color, Filled/Unfilled)` Draws a circle given its center (X,Y) and its radius.
ellipse	`Draw_Ellipse(X1, Y1, X2, Y2, Color, Filled/Unfilled)` Draws an ellipse inscribed in the rectangle defined by two diagonally opposite corners, (X1,Y1) and (X2,Y2), of the specified color.
arc	`Draw_Arc(X1, Y1, X2, Y2, Startx, Starty, Endx, Endy, Color)` Draws a portion of the ellipse that is inscribed inside the rectangle defined by two diagonally opposite corners, (X1,Y1) and (X2,Y2), of the specified color.
single pixel	`Put_Pixel(X,Y,Color)` Sets a single pixel to the specified color.
fill a closed region	`Flood_Fill(X, Y, Color)` Fills a closed region containing the specified (X,Y) coordinate with the specified color. (If the region is not closed, this will possibly color the entire window.)
draw text	`Display_Text(X, Y, Text, Color)` Draws the characters in the text string, where the (X,Y) location is the upper-left corner of the first drawn character. Text is always drawn from left to right, horizontally across the window.
draw a number as text	`Display_Number(X, Y, Number, Color)` Draws a string of characters that represent the value of Number, where the (X,Y) location is the upper-left corner of the first drawn character.

The basic colors available in RAPTOR are:

White	Black	Red	Blue	Green	Brown	Cyan	Magenta
Yellow	Light_Gray	Dark_Gray	Light_Blue	Light_Green	Light_Cyan	Light_Red	Light_Magenta

The RAPTOR flowchart in Figure 3-5 demonstrates the use of some of these drawing procedures. Notice how the coordinate system is used to not only specify the position of the object but also its size and shape.

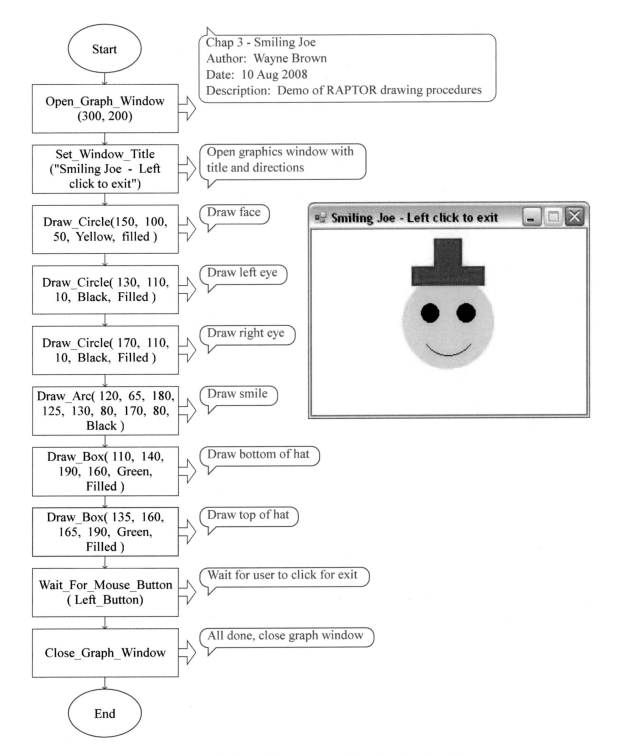

Figure 3-5: RAPTOR Graphics Program that uses a Variety of Procedures and Resulting Graphics Output

Two of the basic drawing procedures, **Draw_Arc** and the **Flood_Fill,** are a bit more involved than the others and require additional explanation.

The **Draw_Arc** procedure draws a portion of an ellipse. We must specify a bounding box that defines the limits of the entire ellipse. The arc that is drawn starts at the intersection point of the ellipse with a line from the center of the ellipse to the point (Startx, Starty). The arc ends at the intersection of the ellipse with a line from the center to the point (Endx, Endy). The arc is always drawn in a counter-clockwise direction. Only the red line in the example below was drawn by a **Draw_Arc** procedure. Figure 3-6 demonstrates this concept and show the RAPTOR code that produced it.

Draw_Arc(X1, Y1, X2, Y2, Startx, Starty, Endx, Endy, Color)

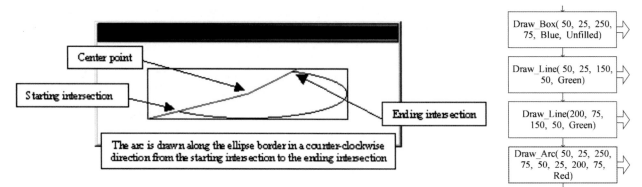

Figure 3-6: Example Use of the Draw_Arc Procedure

When we need a "non-standard" shape, we can use a series of **Draw_Line** and other drawing commands to totally enclose the shape's region and then **Flood_Fill** the enclosed region with a desired color by specifying a location inside of the enclosed area. The color used to draw the boundary must be different from the **Flood_Fill** color. You must be careful when using a flood fill command because, if the area is not totally enclosed, the fill will "leak" out and possibly fill the entire graphics window. Figure 3-7 provides an example use of **Flood_Fill** and the RAPTOR code that produced it.

Flood_Fill(X, Y, Color)

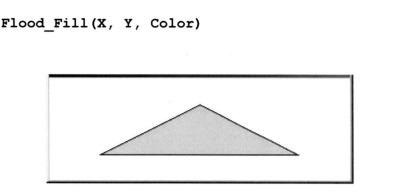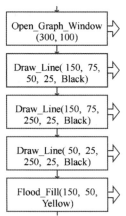

Figure 3-7: Example Use of the Flood_Fill Procedure

Up until now we have drawn all of our shapes at very specific locations defined by numbers. We could alternatively use variables to hold the locations of numbers and then draw the objects at the locations specified by the variables. For example, we could draw a circle centered at a position given by variables X and Y with the following:

Draw_Circle(X, Y, 10, Red, Filled)

We could also use expressions involving variables to determine where to draw objects such as the following square which is centered at the location given by X and Y (note there is nothing special about X and Y, they are simply what we chose to name our variables):

Draw_Box(X–10, Y–10, X+10, Y+10, Blue, Filled)

To take this idea a bit further and combine it with the **Draw_Arc** and **Flood_Fill** procedures that we discussed earlier, we could create more interesting shapes like the UFO (Unidentified Flying Object) shown in Figure 3-8.

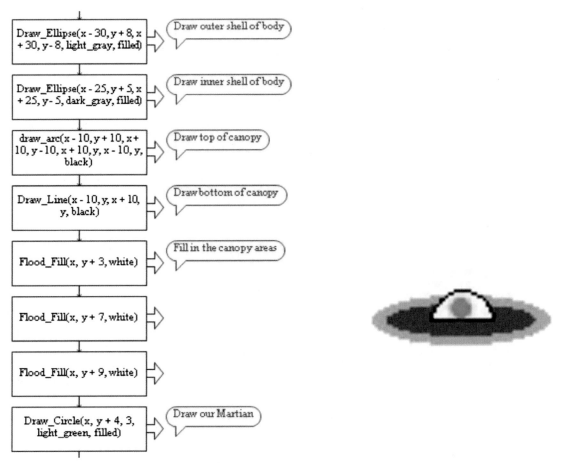

Figure 3-8: RAPTOR Graphics Symbols that use Parameters to Draw a UFO

Interacting with the Graphics Window

Users can interact with the graphics window using either the mouse or the keyboard. A variety of built-in procedures and functions are available for controlling these interactions. The procedures are invoked

33

with a Call symbol, just like the drawing procedures were in the previous section. Procedures do not return values, but they can modify the variables that are included as their parameters. For example, the **Get_Mouse_Button(Left_Button, X_Loc, Y_Loc)** procedure places the location of the left mouse button click into the variables X_Loc and Y_Loc.

Functions on the other hand, always return a value and are used in the "To:" (right side) of Assignment symbols but not in a Call symbol. Sqrt() is a function because it returns a number which is the square root of the argument passed to it. An example of a graphics function call would be the **Get_Mouse_X** and **Get_Mouse_Y** functions which return the current X and Y positions of the mouse, respectively.

Another issue with the mouse and keyboard interaction procedures and functions is whether or not they **Block**; that is, when they are called, do they wait for user action (blocking) or do they immediately return a value (nonblocking). The **Get_Mouse_Button(Left_Button, X_Loc, Y_Loc)** procedure blocks and waits for the user to click the left mouse button. The **Get_Mouse_X** and **Get_Mouse_Y** functions do not block but rather immediately give us the current X and Y locations of the mouse, respectively.

The tables 3-1, 3-2, 3-3, and 3-4 provide details on the primary mouse and keyboard interaction procedures and functions available in RAPTOR.

Table 3-1: Nonblocking RAPTOR Mouse Input Procedures and Functions

Nonblocking Mouse Input	Procedure/Function Call With Description
get the X coordinate value of the mouse cursor location	`x ← Get_Mouse_X` A function that returns the X coordinate of the current mouse location. It is typically used in an Assignment construct to save the X location into a variable for later use.
get the Y coordinate value of the mouse cursor location	`y ← Get_Mouse_Y` A function that returns the Y coordinate of the current mouse location. It is typically used in an Assignment construct to save the X location into a variable for later use.
is a mouse button down?	`Mouse_Button_Down(Which_Button)` A function that returns true if the mouse button is down right now.
was a mouse button down?	`Mouse_Button_Pressed(Which_Button)` A function that returns true if the mouse button has been pressed since the last call to Get_Mouse_Button or Wait_For_Mouse_Button. This is often used to test whether or not to call Get_Mouse_Button.
was a mouse button up?	`Mouse_Button_Released(Which_Button)` A function that returns true if the mouse button has been released since the last call to Get_Mouse_Button or Wait_For_Mouse_Button.

Table 3-2: Blocking RAPTOR Mouse Input Procedures

Blocking Mouse Input	Procedure Call With Description
wait for the press of a mouse button	`Wait_For_Mouse_Button(Which_Button)` A procedure that simply waits until the specified mouse button (either `Left_Button` or `Right_Button`) is pressed.
wait for the press of a mouse button	`Get_Mouse_Button(Which_Button, X, Y)` A procedure that takes a button (either `Left_Button` or `Right_Button`) and returns the coordinates of a click of that button. If no click is ready to be processed, it waits until the user presses the desired button.

Table 3-3: Nonblocking RAPTOR Keyboard Input Function

Non-blocking Keyboard Input	Function Call With Description
see if a user has pressed a key	`Key_Hit` A function returning the Boolean value True if a key has been pressed since the last call to Get_Key. As a function, it is used in the "to" portion of an Assignment Statement or in Decision blocks (diamonds).

Table 3-4: Blocking RAPTOR Keyboard Input Functions and Procedures

Blocking Keyboard Input	Procedure/Function Call With Description
wait for the press of a key	`Wait_For_Key` A procedure that simply waits until a keyboard key is pressed.
get a user key press	`Character_variable ←Get_Key` A function that returns the character typed by the user. If no character is ready to be processed, Get_Key waits until the user presses a key.
get a user key press, even if it is a special character like 'home'	`String_variable ← Get_Key_String` A function that returns string that describes the type pressed by the user. If no character is ready to be processed, Get_Key_String waits until the user presses a key. (See the help screens for details.)

With the mouse and keyboard interaction procedures and functions now available to us, we can make our graphics more interactive and interesting. Our next algorithm will:

Draw a circle with a random color wherever the mouse is currently located until the user hits a key.

With this narrative problem statement, we follow our algorithmic reasoning process to first understand the problem statement. This problem is still fairly simple, so there is not much to review. Next, we create our design as the list of tasks shown below.

35

- Open a graphics window with title and directions displayed
- Loop through the following steps until a key is hit
  - Get the current mouse location
  - Draw a circle of random color at that location
- Close the graphics window and exit

The flowchart in Figure 3-9 implements this algorithm.

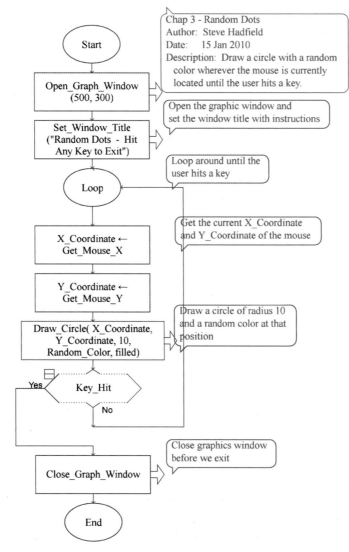

Figure 3-9: Random Dots Algorithm

The next few sentences will review the flowchart and make sure we cover all the necessary steps as is common in the Test step. The Loop construct repeatedly gets the mouse location and draws a circle there. The loop includes an exit condition that uses the **Key_Hit** function to check if a key has been hit and exits the loop if one has (we'll learn more about loops in a few more chapters). Repeated within the loop are two Assignment symbols with the **Get_Mouse_X** and **Get_Mouse_Y** functions to obtain the X and Y locations of the mouse and save them in variables **x** and **y**, respectively. The **Draw_Circle** procedure uses these variables to know where to draw the circle. The **Random_Color** parameter to

Draw_Circle is actually a built-in function that returns a randomly chosen color. Figure 3-10 provides an example from the running the Random Dots flowchart.

Figure 3-10: Example Run of the Random Dots Program

To further practice some algorithmic reasoning within RAPTOR's graphics capabilities, let's solve another problem. Specifically, we will:

Draw a non-trivial object at the locations where the user clicks until they hit a key to exit.

Following our problem solving process, we first review the problem statement to understand the goal. Then we create a design by coming up with the list of tasks below.

- Open a graphics window with appropriate title and directions
- Loop through the following steps until the user hits a key
  - Check if the user has left-clicked the mouse and if so:
    - Get the mouse click location
    - Draw the non-trivial object at that location (we'll draw the UFO from earlier)
- Close graphics window and exit

Based upon this design, the RAPTOR flowchart in Figure 3-11 implements this algorithm. For the test step, we will carefully review what this flowchart does and then have some fun by running it producing same output as shown in Figure 3-12.

The Loop is controlled in the same way as our Random Dots flowchart, with an exit when the user hits a key. Within the loop, there is now a check that determines if the left mouse button has been pressed. If it has, then **Get_Mouse_Button(Left_Button, x, y)** is called to get that location. The **Draw_UFO** procedure knows to draw a UFO at the position specified by the **x** and **y** variables. Draw_UFO is a procedure that the author implemented for you and which we'll learn to do ourselves later. Below is a sample run of the flowchart.

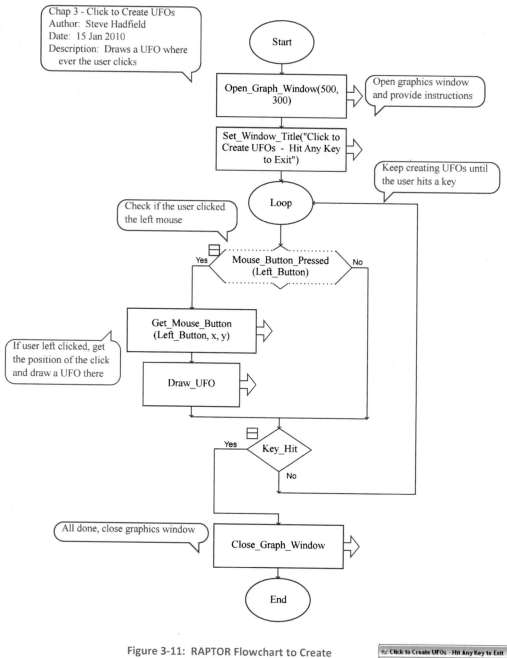

Chap 3 - Click to Create UFOs
Author: Steve Hadfield
Date: 15 Jan 2010
Description: Draws a UFO where
ever the user clicks

Start

Open_Graph_Window(500, 300)

Open graphics window and provide instructions

Set_Window_Title("Click to Create UFOs - Hit Any Key to Exit")

Keep creating UFOs until the user hits a key

Loop

Check if the user clicked the left mouse

Mouse_Button_Pressed (Left_Button)

Yes   No

Get_Mouse_Button (Left_Button, x, y)

If user left clicked, get the position of the click and draw a UFO there

Draw_UFO

Key_Hit

Yes   No

All done, close graphics window

Close_Graph_Window

End

Figure 3-11: RAPTOR Flowchart to Create Multiple Objects

Figure 3-12: Sample Run of Multiple Objects Program

38

Conclusion

RAPTOR provides simple, yet powerful graphics capabilities through the RAPTORGraph library of procedures and functions. The procedures are used via RAPTOR's Call Symbol. The functions can be executed from within the To: part of an Assignment symbol, in a Loop exit condition, or in a Selection condition. Together RAPTOR's graphical capabilities and mouse/keyboard controls allow us to create interesting and interactive graphical programs.

Exercises

1. Write an algorithm to create your own complex shape, like we did with the UFO.

2. Modifies our algorithm that draws random circles to draw random squares instead. What else do you have to do to make this algorithm work that you did not have to do when drawing circles?

3. Recreate the Random Dots algorithm from Figure 3.9 and add a Call to Clear_Window() inside the look so only the dot at the latest mouse position is shown.

4. Create an algorithm similar to the Create Multiple Objects algorithm in Figure 3.11, but have your algorithm draw some other complex shape, instead of the UFO.

5. **CHALLENGE EXERCISE**: Create an algorithm similar to the Create Multiple Objects algorithm in Figure 3.11, but have your algorithm draw one type of complex shape upon a right click of the mouse and a different complex shape upon a left click of the mouse. Be creative and make the complex shapes whatever you want.

4. Selection: Adding Decision-Making to Algorithms

Up to this point most of our flowcharts have been sequential in nature with symbols only executed one after another. However, algorithms frequently need to be able to change what is done next based on current conditions. For example, if an item is on sale, a point-of-sale terminal (automated cash register) would need to calculate the price differently than for non-sale items. To accomplish this type of control flow, RAPTOR includes the Selection construct shown in Figure 4-1.

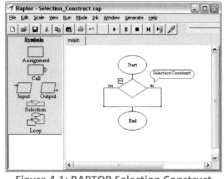

Figure 4-1: RAPTOR Selection Construct

Selection Construct

The key to the Selection construct is the diamond shape that occurs in the top center. In that diamond, we put an expression that evaluates to either Yes (True) or No (False). If it evaluates to Yes, the Yes branch on the left is followed to determine the next symbol to evaluate. If the expression evaluates to No, the No branch on the right is followed. On both the left (Yes) and the right (No) branches, we can include any of the RAPTOR symbols, including additional Selections.

Decision Expressions

The decision expressions that go within the diamond of the Selection construct are expressions that evaluate to a value of Yes (True) or No (False). These expressions, also called Boolean expressions, can be built in the following ways:

- Relational comparisons such as X < 7, Y = 4, Z >= (Y+3), A != 9, Name = "Sally", Name < "Bob".
- Functions that return True or False like Key_Hit, Is_Number(), Mouse_Button_Pressed(Left_Button).
- Logical expressions using And, Or, Not, and XOR like (X > 7) And (Y = 4), (X=5) Or Not(Key_Hit).

These new operators are further explained in Table 4-1.

Table 4-1: RAPTOR's Relational and Logical Operators

Operator	Description	Example
=	"is equal to"	3 = 4 is No (False)
!=	"is not equal to"	3 != 4 is Yes (True)
/=		3 /= 4 is Yes (True)
<	"is less than"	3 < 4 is Yes (True)
<=	"is less than or equal to"	3 <= 4 is Yes (True)
>	"is greater than"	3 > 4 is No (False)
>=	"is greater than or equal to"	3 >= 4 is No (False)
Not	Yes (True) only if **what follows is False**	Not (3 < 4) is No (False)
And	Yes (True) if **both** are Yes	(3 < 4) And (10 < 20) is Yes (True)
XOR	Yes (True) only if **one side is True but the other is not**	(3 < 4) XOR (10 < 20) is No(False)
Or	Yes (True) if **either** are Yes	(3 < 4) Or (10 > 20) is Yes(True)

Decision expressions can be built with arithmetic expressions, like we have seen for the Assignment symbol, within them, as long as the final result is a Yes/No (True/False). For example, we could have a decision expression like:

$$Sqrt(\ (X1-X2)^2 + (Y1-Y2)^2\ ) < 5$$

to test if the distance between the points (X1, Y1) and (X2, Y2) is less than 5. This begs the question, "Which parts of the expression are evaluated before the others?" The "order of precedence" for evaluating a decision expression, similar to the order of precedence for an assignment expression from Chapter 2, is shown below; however, it is always best to use parentheses to explicitly control the order of evaluation.

1. compute all functions, then
2. compute anything in parentheses, then
3. compute exponentiation (^,**) i.e., raise one number to a power, then
4. compute multiplications and divisions, left to right, then
5. compute additions and subtractions, left to right, then
6. evaluate relational operators (= != /= < <= > >=), left to right,
7. evaluate any **Not** logical operators, left to right,
8. evaluate any **And** logical operators, left to right,
9. evaluate any **XOR** logical operators, left to right, then finally,
10. evaluate any **Or** logical operators, left to right.

The relational operators, (=, !=, /=, <, <=, >, >=), must always compare two values of the same types of data (either numbers, text strings, or "yes/no" values). For example, 3 = 4 and "Wayne" > "Sam" are valid comparisons, but 3 = "Mike" is invalid because it is comparing a number to a text string.

The logical operators, (And , Or, XOR), must always combine two Yes/No (True/False) expressions into a single Yes/No value. The logical operator Not must always convert a single Yes/No value into its opposite value. Several valid and invalid examples of decision expressions are shown in Table 4-2.

Table 4-2: Decision Expression Examples

Example	Valid or Invalid?
(3<4) And (10<20)	Valid
(flaps_angle < 30) And (air_speed < 120)	Valid, assuming flaps_angle and air_speed both contain numerical data.
5 And (10<20)	Invalid - the left side of the "And" is a number, not a Yes/No (True/False) value.
5 <= x <= 7	Invalid - because the 5 <= x is evaluated into a Yes/No value and then the evaluation of that Yes/NO as <= 7 is an invalid relational comparison.

To help clarify our use of the Selection construct, we will look at a couple of examples. In the first example (Figure 4-2), if a student has made the Dean's List (GPA greater than or equal to 3.0), then a congratulations message will be displayed - otherwise nothing is displayed (since the "no" branch is empty). This is called an If-Then selection because "if" the condition is true, "then" we do something.

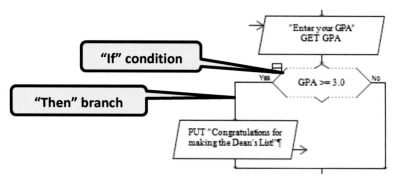

Figure 4-2: Dean's List If-Then Selection

In the next example (Figure 4-3), one line of text is always displayed, with the value of the GPA variable determining which one. We call this an If-Then-Else selection as the "no" branch handles the "else" condition.

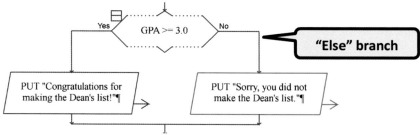

Figure 4-3: Dean's List If-Then-Else Selection

Cascading Selection Constructs

A single selection-control statement can make a choice between one or two choices. If we need to make a decision that involves more than two choices, we need to have multiple selection control constructs. For example, if we are assigning a letter grade (A, B, C, D, or F) based on a numeric score, we need to select between five choices, as shown in Figure 4-4. This is sometimes referred to as "cascading selection construct," because it resembles water cascading over a series of waterfalls.

For a Score of 85, we take the first No branch. Because we are on this No branch we know that Score < 90. So, we need only test that Score >= 80 for the next selection decision in the cascade. This makes for an elegant and efficient algorithm.

Alternatively we could have done this with five Selections, one after the other. But then each one would have needed a complex decision expression such as, " (Score < 90) AND (Score >= 80) ". This approach would be a lot more work with many more chances for making mistakes; and it would take the computer more time to run as each decision expression is more complex and each of the five expressions would be evaluated every time the flow chart is run. With the cascading selection construct, once the appropriate branch is found, nothing more needs to be check.

42

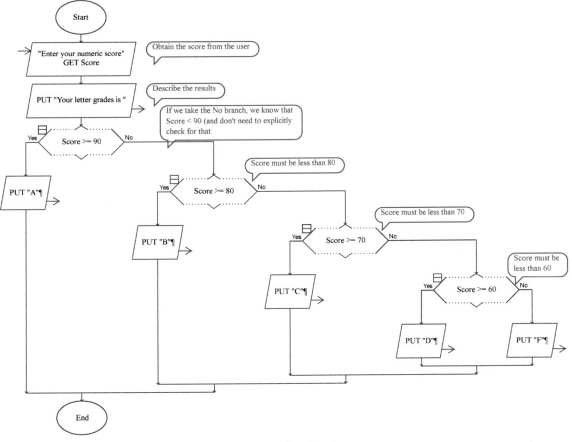

Figure 4-4: Letter Grades Flowchart

Nested Selection Constructs

Another way to combine Selection constructs is to nest them within both sides (branches) of a top level selection. This approach is especially helpful when dealing with selection decisions based on two different variables' values. For example, if we want to determine the quadrant of the X-Y plane that a point falls in, we might create a flowchart like that shown in Figure 4-5. The first Selection of X >= 0 breaks the problem down into two parts, the left and right sides of the Y axis. The Yes branch implies that we must be in quadrants I or IV and the No branch implies that we must be in quadrants II or III. The next Selections simply solve the problems of whether the point is in quadrants I or IV or quadrants II or III, respectively[4].

---

[4] We are ignoring the issue of points directly on the X and Y axes for now but will address this in a later chapter.

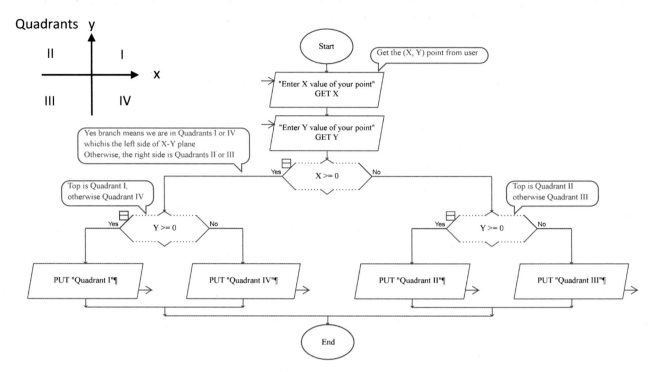

Figure 4-5: (X, Y) Quadrants Flowchart

The key idea behind both cascading and nested Selection constructs is to use them to break complicated decisions into a series of simpler ones. This will make the problem simpler to deal with, easier to test, and less prone to mistakes. For example, the flowchart to determine quadrants above could have been written with four Selections (one right after the next) to test for each quadrant in turn. But doing this would have resulted in the following four rather complicated decision expressions rather than our three simple decision expressions:

(X >=0) And (Y>=0) **for Quadrant I**
(X<0) And (Y>=0) **for Quadrant II**
(X<0) And (Y<0) **for Quadrant III**
(X>=0) And (Y<0) **for Quadrant IV**

Testing Selection Constructs

When testing and debugging selection constructs, we have several approaches to follow: All-Paths, All-Conditions, and Boundary Values.

The **All-Paths technique** uses test inputs that will cause each path through the flowchart to be executed. For the example of the Quadrants program, we would try a point from each of the four quadrants (such as (1,1), (1,-1), (-1,-1), and (1,-1)) to ensure we tried each Yes and each No branch at least once.

With the **All-Conditions technique**, we use test cases that try all combinations of complicated conditions joined together by And, Or, and XOR. For example, the Selection construct to the right has a decision expression with two parts: (X>=0) and (Y>=0) which are joined together with an And. With the All-

Conditions technique we would use test inputs to try all combinations of the two parts being True and False. This technique results in the four test cases shown in Table 4-3.

Table 4-3: All-Conditions Test Cases

X Input	Y Input	(X>=0)	(Y>=0)	(X>=0) And (Y>=0)
2	2	True	True	True
2	-2	True	False	False
-2	2	False	True	False
-2	-2	False	False	False

For the **Boundary Values technique**, we look at the relational expressions (such as (X>=0) in the case above) and use test inputs that are right on the boundaries (thesholds) of the decision. For the (X>=0) expression, we might try values of 0 (zero), -0.01, and 0.01 for X to make sure everything works properly right on the edge of the decision criteria.

If we build our flowcharts in small pieces and test as we go, we will likely catch any problems early when they are simpler to resolve. Testing as we go makes algorithm development an easier, more positive, and more rewarding activity that results in much higher quality algorithms.

Example Problems

With our new found understanding of the Selection construct, we can start to solve more interesting problems and further sharpen our algorithmic reasoning skills. First, let us solve a problem that will involve some string comparisons and nested selections. Specifically, the problem involves determining appropriate total price for a purchase from your online water ski store. The problem statement is:

> **Create an algorithm for determining the total price for a purchase of water skis from your on-line store. If the order will ship to Florida (state is "FL"), then the shipping fee is $20 and we'll give a discount of 10 percent for purchases of 5 or more pairs of skis. For all other states, the shipping fee is $30 and we'll give a discount of 12 percent on purchases of 4 or more pairs of skis.**

Reading through the problem statement, the Understand step of our approach, we realize that there are some details missing such as what information is required as input. We realize that to determine the total price of an order, we will need the unit price of the skis, the quantity of skis ordered, and the destination state. For simplicity, we'll also assume that all purchases will be for only one type of skis and that there is not any sales tax. With these assumptions in mind, we can move on to the Design step of our problem solving process and generate a list of steps to be accomplished:

- Accept inputs of unit price, quantity purchased, and destination state
- If the destination state is Florida then
    - Set shipping fee as $20
    - If the quantity purchased is 5 or more, set the discount to 10 percent
- Otherwise
    - Set shipping fee as $30
    - If the quantity purchased is 4 or more, set the discount to 12 percent
- Calculate total price
- Report total price

Proceeding onto our Implement step, the RAPTOR flowchart in Figure 4-6 is created to implement our design.

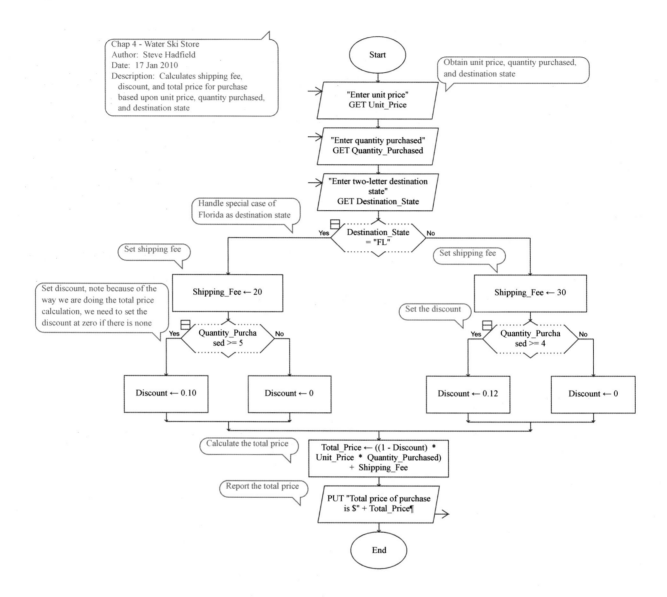

Figure 4-6: Water Ski Store Flowchart

Note the use of a nested Selection construct to distinguish between shipments to Florida and whether or not to apply a discount. We chose to set variables within the Selection constructs and then just do the total price calculation at the end based on the values in those variables. We could have done the calculations within the Selection construct and that approach would have worked just as well.

For the Test step, we could construct a number of "test cases" that would exercise each of the paths through our flowchart. We should also be sure to test the "threshold values" which are where the selection conditions change behaviors. For example, the threshold value for Quantity_Purchased when the Destination_State is "FL" is 5, so we would create test cases with Destination_State as "FL" and

46

Quantity_Purchased as 5 and then a separate test case where Quantity_Purchased is 4. Table 4-4 below provides a fairly comprehensive set of test cases for our Water Ski Store program.

Table 4-4: Water Ski Store Test Cases

Test Case #	Unit_Price Input	Quantity_Purchased Input	Destination_ State Input	Expected Total_Price	Notes
1	75.00	2	FL	$170.00	"FL" leftmost branch
2	80.00	7	FL	$524.00	"FL" rightmost branch
3	93.00	2	AZ	$216.00	Non-"FL" left branch
4	78.99	8	NC	$586.09	Non-"FL" right branch
5	55.00	4	FL	$240.00	"FL" lower threshold
6	104.00	5	FL	$488.00	"FL" upper threshold
7	120.88	3	WA	$392.64	Non-"FL" lower threshold
8	93.27	4	ND	$358.31	Non-"FL" upper threshold

Next we will create a graphics algorithm that uses Selection constructs. We will call this the "Revealed Bull's Eye" program and, for it, we will have the user move the mouse around the graphics window to reveal a hidden image. Here is the problem description:

> **Create a RAPTOR flowchart that will reveal the hidden image of a bull's eye in the graphics window. As the mouse is moved in a 500 x 500 graphics window, draw a red circle if the mouse is within 100 pixels of the center, a green circle if the mouse is 100 pixels or more but less than 200, or a blue circle otherwise.**

After analyzing the problem statement for the Understand step of our approach, we move to the Design step and develop the following set of bullets describing the tasks that need to be accomplished:

- Open a 500 x 500 graphics window with appropriate title and directions
- Loop until the left mouse button is pressed to exit
    - Get the current mouse position
    - Calculate the distance from the current mouse position to the center of the graphics window
    - If the distance is less than 100, draw a red dot of radius 5
    - Otherwise if the distance is less than 200, draw a green dot of radius 5
    - Otherwise draw a blue dot of radius 5
- When the left mouse button is pressed, exit the loop
- Close the graphics window

Proceeding to the Implementation step, we develop the RAPTOR flowchart shown in Figure 4-7 that makes use of a cascading selection construct to determine the appropriate color for the dot at the current mouse location.

The Test step for this program is pretty fun and easy, we simply run the program and move the mouse around checking that the mouse locations are correctly colored. A sample run of this algorithm would produce a display such as is shown in Figure 4-8.

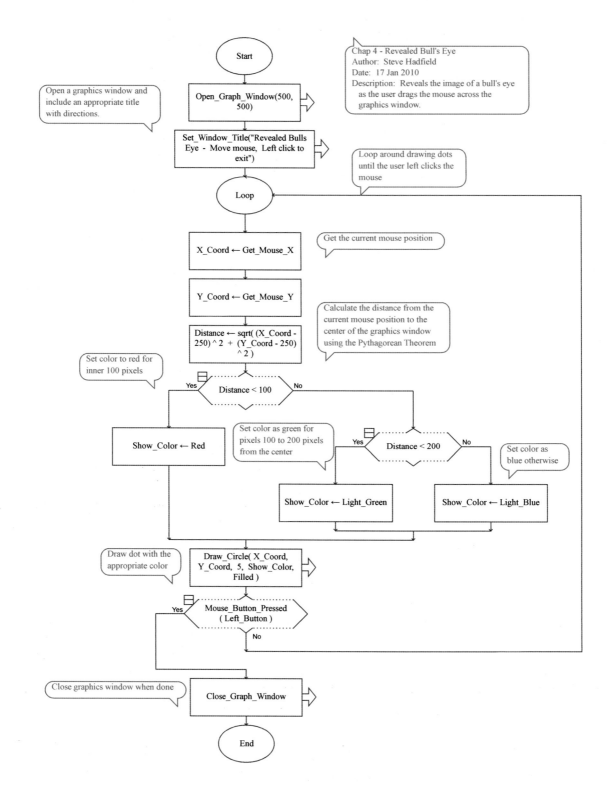

Figure 4-7: Revealed Bull's Eye Flowchart

48

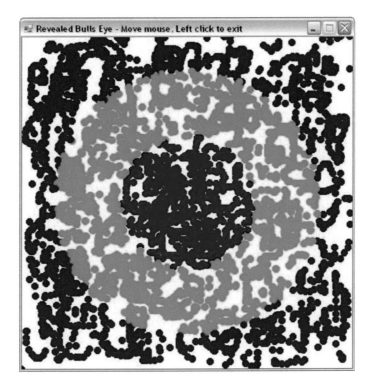

Figure 4-8: Revealed Bull's Eye Sample Output

Conclusion

The Selection construct provides an important new capability when creating algorithms - the ability to choose between alternative paths in our algorithms. The decision, or Boolean, expressions to control these choices can be built from relational and logical operations on values in variables and values returned from function calls. Furthermore, Selection constructs can be nested and cascaded into complex structures such as cascading selections to check a variable for a number of different values or nested selections for checking values in multiple variables.

Exercises

1. Modify our algorithm for purchasing water skis to add another state. If the order will ship to Texas (state is "TX"), then the shipping fee is $10 and we'll give a discount of 10% for orders of 3 or more.

2. Create a RAPTOR flowchart to 'reveal' some image other than the bull's eye from the last example in this chapter. Suggest that you use circles and rectangles to build your image.

3. Write an algorithm that accepts the values for a, b, and c for a quadratic equation as shown below.

$$a\,x^2 + b\,x + c = 0$$

Then calculate and report the roots of the quadratic equation with those coefficients. Recall that the quadratic formal is:

$$x = \frac{-b \pm \sqrt{b^2 - 4\,a\,c}}{2\,a}$$

Note that if the expression $b^2 - 4\,a\,c$ (called the determinant) is positive, there are two real roots.

If the determinant is zero, there is one repeated root, $\frac{-b}{2*a}$.

If it is negative, there are two complex conjugate roots, $\frac{-b}{2*a} + \frac{\sqrt{|b^2-4\,a\,c|}}{2*a}\,i$ and $\frac{-b}{2*a} - \frac{\sqrt{|b^2-4\,a\,c|}}{2*a}\,i.$

4. The table below shows the United States marginal income tax rates for 2017 based upon filing status and annual income. Write an algorithm that accepts the filing status (S for single and M for married) and the annual income and then calculates and reports the marginal tax rate and the tax amount (annual income times the marginal tax rate).

Marginal tax rates for 2017

Marginal Tax Rate	Single Taxable Income	Married Filing Jointly or Qualified Widow(er) Taxable Income
25%	$37,951 – $91,900	$75,901 – $153,100
28%	$91,901 – $191,650	$153,101 – $233,350
33%	$191,651 – $416,700	$233,351 – $416,700
35%	$416,701 – $418,400	$416,701 – $470,700

5. To the right is a scuba dive table from NAUI Worldwide that shows, among other things, the maximum dive time (MDT) for a given dive depth (circled red number) and the diver's letter group (bottom of each column). The diver's letter group determines what their limits would be for subsequent dives. Write an algorithm that accepts a dive depth in feet and then determines and reports the corresponding maximum dive time and the resulting diver's letter group. Reference: https://www.naui.org/resources/dive-tables-review/.

TABLE 1 - END-OF-DIVE LETTER GROUP

5. Loops: Doing Things Over-and-Over Again

Thus far we have learned about the Sequence and Selection control constructs and these have allowed us to create many useful algorithms. However, to complete our toolbox, we need one more control structure: the Loop construct. The Loop construct gives us the ability to do tasks over and over again, greatly increasing the number of problems we can solve. RAPTOR provides a simple, but powerful and flexible Loop construct for use in our flowchart algorithms.

General Loop Construct

RAPTOR's general loop structure is shown in Figure 5-1. There is one entry point at the top (at the Loop circle) and a single exit point at the bottom (following the Exit Condition). The diamond symbol provides the loop exit. We must specify a decision expression for this diamond symbol in the same manner that we did for the Selection construct's diamond. The logic in the exit condition causes the loop to exit when the decision expression evaluates to Yes (True) and thus is an "exit when" condition. If the exit decision expression evaluates to No (False), execution flow goes down and back around to the top of the loop structure and the loop is repeated.

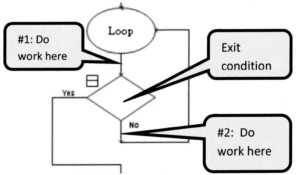

Figure 5-1: RAPTOR's General Loop Construct

We can specify the tasks to accomplish within the Loop construct in two places; the arrow that goes from the Loop circle to the exit condition (indicated with "#1: Do work here." In the diagram above) and then directly below the exit condition (indicate with "#2: Do work here."). The difference in these two regions is that the upper area will always be executed at least once because it occurs before the exit condition. The lower region is only executed if the loop does not exit.

Input Validation Loop

The phrase "Garbage In – Garbage Out" refers to the idea that if bad information is provided as input to an algorithm, the results will likely be bad as well. A well designed algorithm will protect against this happening by only allowing valid information to be provided as input. The Loop construct is ideal for input validation and can be set up to repeat until valid input is provided.

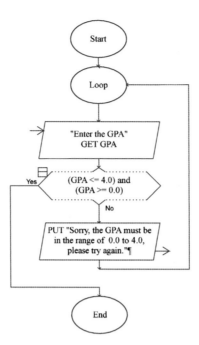

Figure 5-2: Initial GPA Input Validation Loop

Take, for example, the need to input a grade point average which must be in the range of 0.0 to 4.0. We could develop the loop shown in Figure 5-2 to ensure a proper value is entered. In this loop, we obtain the GPA from the user before the exit condition check. The exit condition then checks to see if the GPA was valid and, if so, exits the loop. If the GPA is not valid, an error message is displayed and the loop is repeated allowing the user to try again.

While this loop ensures that any number the user might enter is in the correct range, the user could enter a text string, such as "foo", which would cause problems. To fully protect the GPA input, we would need to ensure the input is a number as well. We could do this with a more complex exit condition that includes

Is_Number(GPA)

which is a function call that returns Yes (True) if the value in the GPA variable is a number and No (False) otherwise. Note it is important to check that GPA is a number before the other comparisons because those comparisons assume that GPA is a number. For this reason, the Is_Number() must be in the leftmost part of the decision expression. This improved GPA Input validation loop is shown in Figure 5-3.

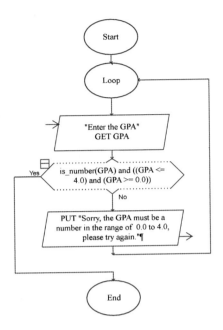

Figure 5-3: Improved GPA Input Validation Loop

This example is starting to get a bit complicated and certainly there are more complex input validation conditions that one can imagine. A more flexible way to deal with complex input validation conditions is to do the validation checks before the exit condition and set a **flag** variable to indicate if the input is valid or not. We can then use the flag variable to determine if we should exit the loop. A **flag** variable is simply a variable that holds a Yes/No value which was set in one place but will be used in another. In Figure 5-4 is another version of our GPA input validation flowchart which uses the **GPA_Valid** flag variable. Notice how we added a set of selection statements to our data entry to determine if the flag stays False or is set to True.

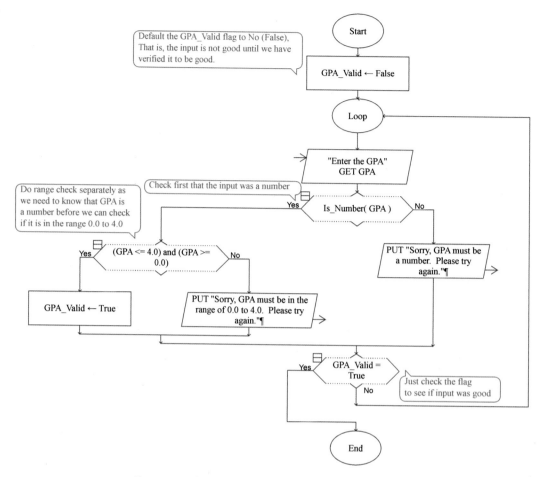

Figure 5-4: Flag-Based Input Validation Loop

Counted Loop Structure

Another common use of the Loop construct is the **Counted Loop**. With Counted Loops, the loop executes a specified number of times and an **index** variable is used to keep track of which iteration of the loop we are on. The format of the counted loop that we will use is the **ITEM Loop,** where **ITEM** stands for **I**nitialize – **T**est – **E**valuate – **M**odify. There are other forms of counted loops but the ITEM loop is both common and flexible. A sample ITEM loop is shown in Figure 5-5. We use the index variable of "i" not because it is terribly descriptive, but because it is a commonly accepted convention (and easy to type).

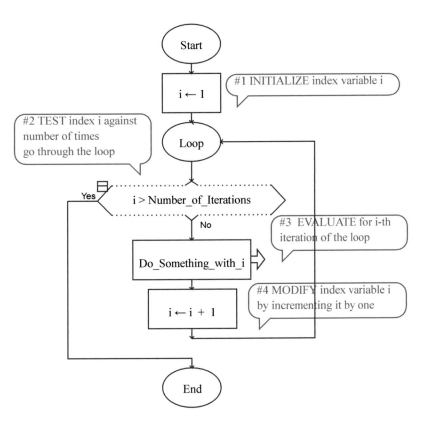

Figure 5-5: ITEM Loop Description

Before the loop, we **Initialize** the index variable (#1), **Test** the index for the exit condition (#2), **Evaluate** whatever we are doing inside the loop (#3), and finally **Modify** the index for the next iteration (#4). Note that the exit condition checks for our index variable **i** being greater than the number of times we want to go through the loop. This works because the last time we go through the loop, we increment **i** which makes it one more than the number of iterations. Another benefit of the ITEM loop is that we will not do the Evaluate part at all if the **Number_Of_Iterations** is zero. *Note, we are assuming that the **Number_Of_Iterations** variable was already set to some specific value.*

To illustrate use of the ITEM counted loop, the flowchart in Figure 5-6 calculates the total and average of a number of input values. First, the flowchart asks for the number of input values to obtain and stores this number in the **Number_of_Inputs** variable. Then, the **Total** variable is initialized to zero. As we input each value, we will add it to this Total variable to keep a running sum of the values. Next, we start the ITEM loop using the index variable **i**. The Evaluate part of the loop has an Input symbol to get the next input value (notice the use of the index variable, i, in the prompt) and an Assignment symbol to add this value to the running **Total**. After the loop, the final value of **Total** is reported and the **Average** is calculated and reported.

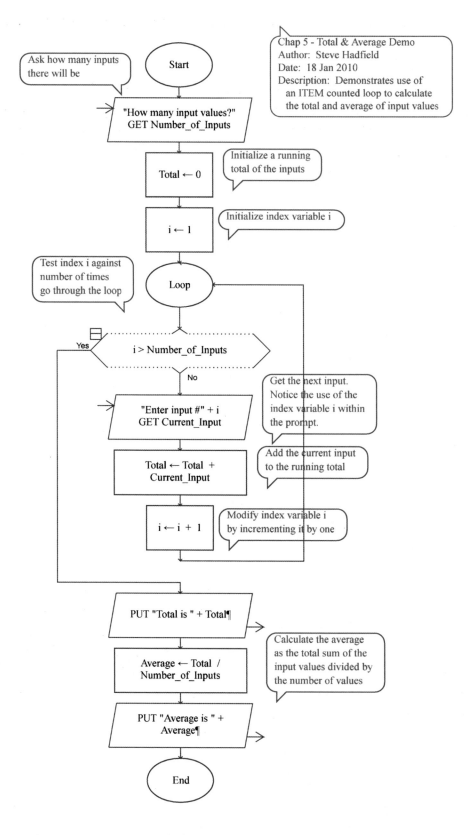

Figure 5-6: ITEM Loop to Calculate the Total and Average of Multiple Inputs

Now we can practice our algorithmic reasoning skills with a loop problem. The problem statement is:

Find the lowest score among a user-specified number of scores.

In reviewing the problem statement (our Understand step), we can identify that to accomplish it we will use a variable to hold the current minimum and compare it to each value read in. If the new value is lower, we'll simply make it the new minimum. Creating a design for this, we come up with the list of tasks below (our Design step):

- Ask the user how many scores there will be
- Set the current lowest score to a value larger than any of the real values
- Loop for each of the specified number of values
    - Read in the next value
    - Compare the next value to the current lowest, if this value is lower:
        - Set the current lowest value to the value just read in
- At the end of the loop, all input scores will have been checked and the current lowest is the least of all of them, so we output the current lowest

Moving onto the Implementation step, we create the flowchart in Figure 5-7. Note that we initialize the **Current_Min** variable to 101 assuming that all the scores will be in the range 0 to 100. This way we are assured that Current_Min will be reset when any valid value is entered.

If we did not know the range of values ahead of time, we could initialize the **Current_Min** variable to the first value that was read in.

Redirect Input / Output

When working with looping algorithms, there may be a great deal of input and we would have to type in each input value every time we ran the flowchart. This can be tedious and prone to errors. Fortunately, there is another option. The **Redirect_Input** procedure takes in a file name as a string argument and then reads input from that file. You can also pass Yes or No to **Redirect_Input** to turn it on or off, respectively. For output, **Redirect_Output** works in a similar manner to send the output to a specified file instead of the Master Console. **Redirect_Output_Append** is similar but instead of overwriting the file, it will append the results to the end of the file. The flowchart in Figure 5-8 demonstrates use of these procedures and also shows the use of counters to keep track of how many input values there were and how many of them were equal to five. Note the use of the **End_Of_Input** function as a loop exit condition to determine when to end the input loop.

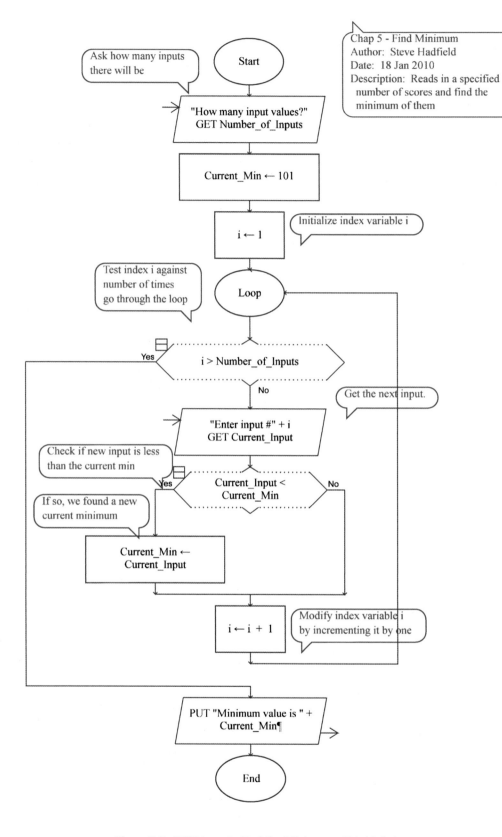

Figure 5-7: ITEM Loop to Find the Minimum of Multiple Inputs

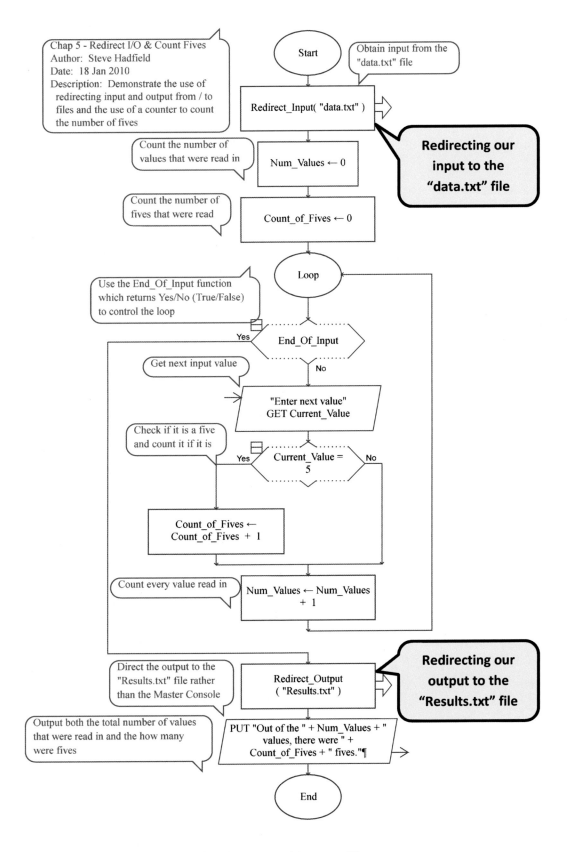

Figure 5-8: Redirecting Input and Output to Files

59

Nested Loops

Just like we nested Selections inside of each other, we can also nest loops inside of each other. To demonstrate, we will use a flowchart that generates a simple multiplication table. The outer loop takes us through the rows of the table and the inner loop takes us through the columns. The variables, **Row** and **Col,** index the two loops and keep track of the current row and column, respectively.

The flowchart in Figure 5-9 uses nested loops to create a multiplication table.

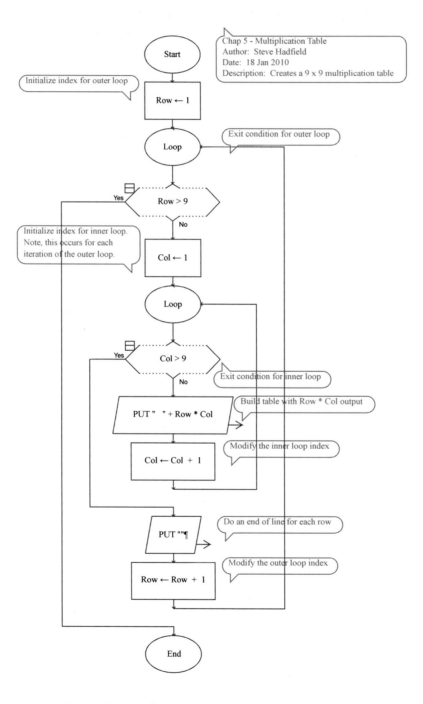

Figure 5-9: Nested Loops to Create a Multiplication Table

The last example flowchart in this chapter (Figure 5-10) accepts an input string and converts it character by character to the ASCII code for that character. Each character and its corresponding ASCII code are shown on a separate line. With this flowchart we see that we can reference the i-th character in a string via:

String_Name[i]

where the "[i]" gives us the i-th character in the string, rather than the whole string. The **length_of()** function tells us how many characters are in the string and helps us determine how many times to go through the loop. The **to_ascii()** function translates a character into the equivalent ASCII numeric code.

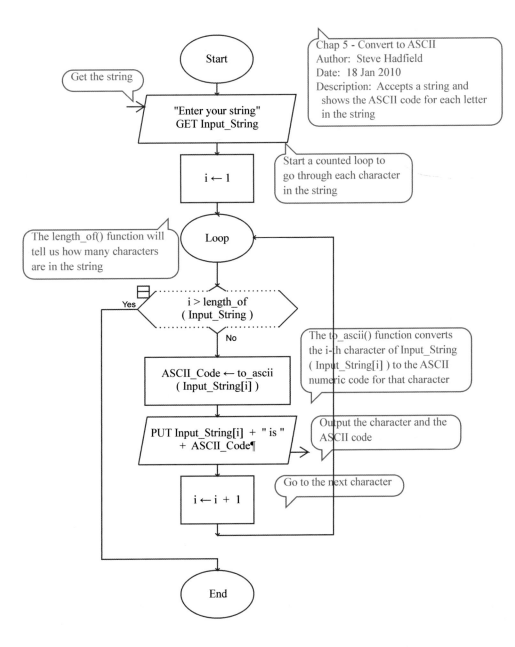

Figure 5-10: Convert to ASCII Flowchart

61

Testing and Debugging Loops

When testing and debugging loops in flowcharts, we want to try to develop test input that will cause the loop to iterate:

- Zero times
- One time
- Maximum number of times minus one
- Maximum number of times
- Maximum number of times plus one (which it should not do)

Depending on the loop, these may or may not be possible to test, but they are a good place to start.

A frequent problem that comes up with the Loop construct is the "Off-By-One" error where the loop will repeat one too many or one too few times. We should take care to check for errors of this nature.

Conclusion

In this chapter we learned about the Loop construct for repeating a process over-and-over again. We saw the general Loop structure in RAPTOR and explored how it can be used by adding additional symbols both before and after the exit condition. Furthermore, we studied the ITEM (Initialize-Test-Evaluate-Modify) method for building a counted loop. We also explored other features of RAPTOR, like the ability to redirect input and output from and to files, and the ability to use an index to access specific characters within a string. The examples also demonstrated how to use loops to sum values, calculate an average, find a minimum, and count occurrences. These techniques will all be useful in the remaining chapters and also in our development of algorithmic reasoning using RAPTOR.

Exercises

1. Modify our algorithm for finding the lowest score to find the highest score. What did you have to do differently?

2. Write an algorithm that accepts a number in the range of 1 to 25 and then counts from 0 to 100 in increments of the input number. For example, an input of 20 would produce: 20, 40, 60, 80, 100.

3. Write an algorithm that accepts 10 scores and reports the minimum, maximum, and average scores. Use a separate input validation loop so that the only scores in the range from 0 to 100, inclusive, are accepted for the 10 input scores. When bad scores, such as -5 and 102 are entered, be sure to provide an appropriate error message giving the range of acceptable scores. You may assume that all inputs are numbers.

4. The Multiplication Table example program in this chapter was designed to show how one can nest loops within each other. However, the table that it produced was not nicely formatted. Update this algorithm so that the columns line up and are nicely presented. Also label the columns and rows with the number (1-9) with which they correspond.

5. Write an algorithm that accepts a sentence as a string input and then counts and reports how many words are in the string. Distinguish words by locating space characters (ASCII code 32) as the break between words. Use a character counter to count the number of characters in each word and use it as a means to deal appropriately with sentences that start with a space, multiple consecutive spaces, and the last words of a sentence.

6. **CHALLENGE EXERCISE**: Create a text file with student names and test scores alternating on separate lines as shown below. Write an algorithm that reads the names and scores from the file, reports the names of any students that scored 100, counts and reports how many students scored 90 or above, and determines and reports the maximum score, the minimum score, and the average score.

```
Sally
100
Bill
85
Gwen
98
Dave
93
George
59
```

6. Analyzing Requirements: Making Clear What the User Wants

Having now learned about all of the symbols and control constructs of RAPTOR flowcharts, we are ready to solve some more complex problems. The first step in successful problem solving, as discussed in our problem solving approach, is to gain a full understanding of the problem to be solved. Unfortunately, this Understand step is often under-appreciated and not adequately addressed, which leads to serious and costly issues as the problem solving effort progresses.

To help to avoid such issues, we will look at a few easy and simple methods to assist us in analyzing and understanding the requirements of the problem at hand. With this understanding, we will be able to develop a complete and effective solution.

The methods and tools that we will discuss in this section are:

- Extracting key points from the problem description, to include inputs, process tasks, and outputs
- Asking probing questions to expose unstated requirements
- Making a lists of tasks to be accomplished and data (variables) that will be needed
- Drawing pictures and creating story boards describing the user interface
- Using decision tables to clarify complex choices

Extracting Key Points

Our very first step in gaining a full understanding of the problem will be to carefully read and decompose the problem statement and to do so several times. The goal of the first reading is to obtain a high-level understanding of the entire problem, so we should read it from start to finish. We could then read it a second time with a pencil and paper at the ready. In this second reading, we would examine each sentence one at a time making note of the following:

- Inputs to be obtained from the user
- Processing tasks to be accomplished
- Outputs to be provided
- Data items and objects (that will likely need to become variables in our algorithm)

To illustrate this, let us consider the problem statement below:

> **Write an algorithm to obtain product orders from customers and price the orders for the customers. The pricing shall apply bulk purchase discounts and state tax rates. The algorithm needs to provide the user with an echo of their inputs together with the discount, tax, and total price.**

Our first read of the problem statement tell us that we need to build an algorithm to price out product orders for customers that include bulk order discounts and state tax rates.

Re-reading the first sentence, we realize that we are going to need to **input** product order information from the customer, **calculate** the price of the order, and **report** the price information to the customer. The detailed read of the second sentence tells us that we will need to calculate **bulk purchase discounts**

64

and apply **state tax rates**. From the third sentence, we surmise that the output must include **product order information, discount, tax,** and **total price**.

Putting this all together, we come up with the following summary of requirements for the problem:

Table 6-1: Initial Input-Process-Output with Variables

Inputs	Processing	Outputs	Variables
Order Information	Obtain inputs Calculate order price - Determine discount - Compute state tax Report results	Order Information Discount Tax Total price	Type of product Product price Quantity ordered Discount Tax Total price

We now have a good start on understanding the problem. However, we also are starting to have some questions come up such as, "What exactly is the order information that we must get from the user?" which leads us to the next step in our process, Asking Probing Questions.

Asking Probing Questions

Seldom will we get a full and complete statement of the requirements for the problem to be solved. However, our first step of Extracting Key Points from the problem statement will give us a start and a framework to further develop. Continuing on with our order pricing example, we study the details of the problem's statement from our summary and come up with important questions such as:

- What exactly is the order information that we must get from the user?
- How are bulk discounts determined?
- What states will we get orders from and what are the tax rates for those states?

We would ask these questions and then further elaborate our problem summary with the answers. The answers to some questions might lead to more questions. For example, order information would likely include product type which would lead to the questions of "What product types will be offered and what are their prices?" After we have finished asking probing questions, our problem summary might look more like the elaborated example in Table 6-2 (with new additions highlighted):

Table 6-2: Elaborated Input-Process-Output with Variables

Inputs	Processing	Outputs	Variables
Order Information - Customer name - Customer state - Product type - Quantity ordered	Obtain inputs Calculate order price - Find product price - Determine discount -- No discount for 1-5 -- 10% off for 6-10 -- 20% off for 11 or more - Compute state tax -- Colorado 7% sales tax -- Wyoming 5% sales tax -- Utah 4% sales tax -- New Mexico 5.5% sales tax Report results	Order Information - Customer name - Customer state - Product type - Quantity ordered Discount Tax Total price	Type of product Product price Quantity ordered Discount Tax Total price

List of Tasks and Variables

As we now have a pretty comprehensive understanding of the problem and what needs to be done to solve it, we can begin our Design step and start to identify the tasks that we'll need to do and the variables that we'll need for our algorithm. This step is best accomplished by starting with high-level tasks and then focusing on each high-level task individually and breaking it down into a set of more detailed sub-tasks. This approach, which is formally called **functional decomposition**, allows us to address big problems by breaking them down into manageable pieces and then focusing on just one of those pieces at a time.

A first cut at the List of Tasks for our order pricing example might look something like the list below based upon the Input-Processing-Output table on the previous page:

- Obtain the product order information
- Calculate the order price
- Report the order pricing information

We would then focus on each task separately to further detail what is needed for that task. Doing this for each of the three main tasks above, again using our Input-Processing-Output table, results in the following additional level of sub-tasks:

- Obtain the product order information
  - Input customer name
  - Input customer's state
  - Input product type
  - Input quantity ordered
- Calculate the order price
  - Look up price of the product type
  - Determine the discount based upon the quantity ordered
  - Calculate the order price as (product_price * quantity) * (1-discount)
  - Determine sales tax based upon state and order price
  - Calculate total price of the order
- Report the order pricing information
  - Report order information
  - Report discount
  - Report tax
  - Report total price

Next, we would go through each of the sub-tasks to determine which might need further elaboration. For example, "Input product type" might require that we check that the user input a valid product. Also, the tasks for determining the discount and sales tax need elaboration. We would continue to elaborate lower level sub-tasks as needed until we get to a point where no further elaboration is necessary. The final List of Tasks for our order example is shown on the next page.

In addition to the List of Tasks, we also can develop a list of the variables we will need. Identifying these early and listing them out will help us when we later use our List of Tasks to implement our algorithm. A List of Variables for our order pricing example would be:

Customer_Name	Quantity_Ordered	Order_Price
Customer_State	Product_Price	Sales_Tax
Product_Type	Discount	Total_Price

List of Tasks for the Order Pricing Example:

- Obtain the product order information
    - Input customer name
    - Input customer's state
        - Check that customer's state is either CO, WY, UT, or NM
    - Input product type
        - Check that a valid product type was entered
    - Input quantity ordered
- Calculate the order price
    - Look up price of the product type
        - If product is snow skis, then product price is $300
        - If product is snowboard, then product price is $200
        - If product is snowshoes, then product price is $100
    - Determine the discount based upon the quantity ordered
        - If quantity is 6 to 10, then discount is 10%
        - If quantity ordered is 11 or more, then discount is 20%
    - Calculate the order price as (product_price * quantity) * (1-discount)
    - Determine sales tax based upon state and order price as (order_price * tax_rate)
        - If state is CO, then tax rate is 7%
        - If state is WY, then tax rate is 5%
        - If state is UT, then tax rate is 4%
        - If state is NM, then tax rate is 5.5%
    - Calculate total price of the order as (order_price + sales_tax)
- Report the order pricing information
    - Report order information
        - Output customer's name and state, product type, and quantity ordered
    - Report discount
    - Report tax
    - Report total price

With this List of Tasks and List of Variables, we can begin the Implement step and start writing the algorithm as a RAPTOR flowchart. However, we are going to hold off doing this until Chapter 7 which introduces RAPTOR Subcharts as subcharts will make our flowchart development much more manageable.

Drawing Pictures and Creating Storyboard

When developing algorithms that involve graphics, we can use sketches and pictures to preview the graphics with users and get their feedback on different approaches before committing a lot of effort into developing the real graphical displays. The picture in Figure 6-X previews a potential graphical interface for a Tic-Tac-Toe game.

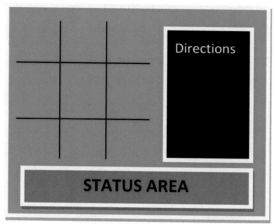

Figure 6-1: Graphical Interface for a Tic-Tac-Toe Game

When the algorithm calls for a series of different graphics or different usages of a primary graphic, we can put together a series of pictures to provide a feel for how the graphics of the algorithm will flow from one view to the next. This series of pictures is called a **storyboard** and is a very common method for algorithm developers to share their visions with future users. The storyboard in Figure 6-2 illustrates a potential flow of the graphical interface for the Tic-Tac-Toe game.

The storyboard above walks through the play of the Tic-Tac-Toe game starting with the welcome screen with directions to the first play by X, then a play by O, and finally to the conclusion of the first game with X winning. In a later chapter, we'll develop an algorithm for this Tic-Tac-Toe game.

Decision Tables for Complex Conditions

When building complex Selection constructs for decision making, especially when they involve multiple variables, the detailed combinations of inputs can get confusing and it becomes easy to misinterpret the specifications, omit details, and run into conflicts. Especially critical are decisions on the boundary values for our decision variables where one thing happens on one side of the boundary and another on the other side. There might even be a third result when exactly on the boundary.

Decision Tables are an excellent tool for dealing with complex decision conditions. A **Decision Table** is a two dimensional table with rows corresponding to ranges of values for one variable and columns corresponding to ranges of values for another variable. To be sure to capture the correct specifications for boundary conditions, we include separate rows and columns for the boundary values.

Back in Chapter 4 on the Selection construct, we worked an example algorithm that would input an (X, Y) point from the user and determine the quadrant in which the point resides. We ignored some boundary conditions where the point could be upon either the X axis and/or the Y axis. Let us come back to this problem and explicitly address these boundary conditions which occur when X equals zero and/or Y equals zero.

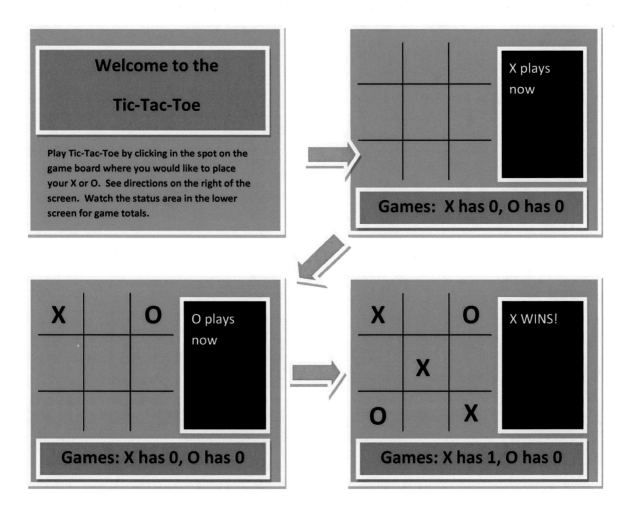

Figure 6-2: Storyboard for a Tic-Tac-Toe Game

The Decision Table for this problem (in Figure 6-3) has three conditions for X as columns and three conditions for Y as rows. In the corresponding entries for various rows and columns are the appropriate classifications of the points, clearly showing the combination of condition on variables X and Y together with the resulting output

	X < 0	X = 0	X > 0
Y > 0	Quadrant II	Y Axis	Quadrant I
Y = 0	X Axis	Origin	X Axis
Y < 0	Quadrant III	Y Axis	Quadrant IV

Figure 6-3: Decision Table for (X, Y) Quadrant Problem

The next step will be to translate this decision table into a corresponding RAPTOR flowchart. This flowchart is rather wide due to all of the Selection constructs. As a result, we will show it in two parts. The first part shows the inputs of X and Y and then roughly half of the needed Selections followed by the final output. The first Selection condition uses the decision condition "**X > 0**" to break the table into two parts: the rightmost column and the leftmost two columns. The first part of the flowchart also shows the additional selections needed for the X > 0 rightmost column of the decision table (see Figure 6-4). With each combination of inputs, the **Location** variable is set with a text string identifying where the point resides. This **Location** variable is then used in the final output.

The second part of the flowchart (Figure 6-5) shows the additional selections needed for the leftmost two columns of the decision table.

Once the flowchart has been created in RAPTOR, we will want to test each of the nine possible cases. To accomplish this we could use the following test inputs: (1, 1), (0, 1), (-1, 1), (-1, 0), (0, 0), (1, 0), (1, -1), (0, -1), and (-1, -1).

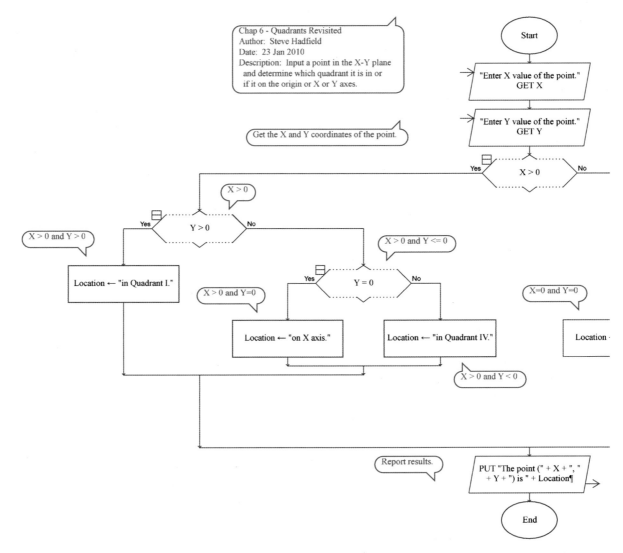

Figure 6-4: First Part of the Revised (X, Y) Quadrant Flowchart

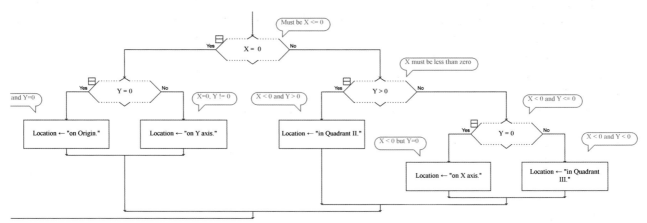

Figure 6-5: Second Part of the Revised (X, Y) Quadrant Flowchart

For a second example of using a decision table to analyze complex decision conditions, we will look at a fire danger rating system. The National Fire Danger Rating System[5] run by the National Oceanic and Atmospheric Administration (NOAA) is a very sophisticated system that uses complex algorithms and a large number of data sources to calculate fire dangers across the United States. The specification below provides a very crude alternative that is simply provided as an example to illustrate the use of decision tables for analyzing complex condition requirements.

Alternative Fire Danger Rating System Specification

> **The fire danger rating shall be determined based upon the forecasted wind speed and the number of inches of rainfall within the past 48 hours. If the wind speed is 10 miles per hour (MPH) or less and there has been at least 1.0 inches of rainfall in the last 48 hours, then the fire danger rating is "Low". If the wind speed is more than 10 MPH and there has been at least 1.0 inches of rainfall, then the rating is "Moderate". The rating is "High" if there has been more than 0.5 inches of rainfall and the wind speed is under 10 MPH. If the wind speed is 10 MPH or more and there has been at least 0.5 inches but less than 1.0 inches of rainfall in the last 48 hours, then the rating is "Very High". Finally, if there has been less than 0.5 inches of rainfall and the wind speed is 10 MPH or more, then the fire danger rating is "Extreme".**

To analyze the requirements provided for the Alternative Fire Danger Rating System, we first read through the entire paragraph and extract the decision variables and the key decision values for these variables. We find that the decision variables are wind speed and rainfall within the last 48 hours. The key decision value for wind speed is 10 miles per hour. The key decision values for recent rainfall are 0.5 inches and 1.0 inches.

We next use these values to build a decision table much like what we did for the quadrants example earlier. The resulting decision table structure is shown in Figure 6-6:

---

[5] Additional information on the National Fire Danger Rating system available at
http://www.srh.noaa.gov/ridge2/fire/.

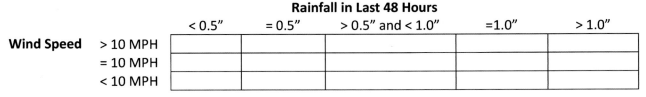

Rainfall in Last 48 Hours

		< 0.5"	= 0.5"	> 0.5" and < 1.0"	=1.0"	> 1.0"
Wind Speed	> 10 MPH					
	= 10 MPH					
	< 10 MPH					

Figure 6-6: Initial (Empty) Decision Table for Fire Danger

With the decision table created using the decision variables and their key values, we carefully re-read the specification one sentence at a time filling in decision table values based upon the information provided in the sentence. For example, the second sentence in the specification states:

> **If the wind speed is 10 miles per hour (MPH) or less and there has been at least 1.0 inches of rainfall in the last 48 hours, then the fire danger rating is "Low".**

From this sentence, we can fill in four entries in our decision table as shown in Figure 6-7:

Rainfall in Last 48 Hours

		< 0.5"	= 0.5"	> 0.5" and < 1.0"	=1.0"	> 1.0"
Wind Speed	> 10 MPH					
	= 10 MPH				Low	Low
	< 10 MPH				Low	Low

Figure 6-7: Fire Danger Decision Table with First Specification Added

We continue to read one sentence of the specification at a time and complete the remainder of the table (see Figure 6-8). Upon completion, we have the decision table shown below. Note, that there are some problems with this table. In particular, two entries have been left unspecified (shown shaded in red) and two have conflicting specifications (shown with diagonal hashes). Finding these omissions and conflicts from the narrative specification would have been very difficult. However, the decision table makes them very apparent.

Rainfall in Last 48 Hours

		< 0.5"	= 0.5"	> 0.5" and < 1.0"	=1.0"	> 1.0"
Wind Speed	> 10 MPH	Extreme	Very High	Very High	Moderate	Moderate
	= 10 MPH	Extreme	Very High	Very High	Low	Low
	< 10 MPH			High	Low / High	Low / High

Figure 6-8: Completed Fire Danger Decision Table

Our next step would be to use this table as a tool to show the customer and get their input as to how best to resolve the omissions and conflicts. However, to help us learn how to create a flowchart to implement a decision table we will proceed with the decision table as-is.

The decision table provides assistance in developing an appropriate combination of Selection constructs to determine the appropriate action. Specifically, we look for natural groupings within the table where we can easily divide it into smaller parts that are easier to address. Once such grouping would occur with the last two columns of the table. The decision condition of "Rainfall < 1.0" would put the first three columns down the left (Yes) branch and the remaining two rightmost columns down the right (No) branch of the Selection construct. See the red and green blocks in Figure 6-9.

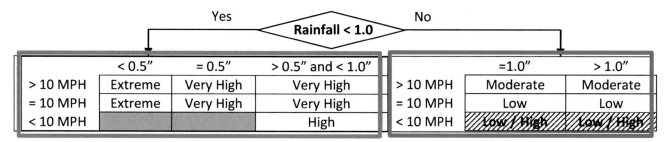

Figure 6-9: First Selection to Implement the Fire Danger Decision Table

The smaller table on the left side (of Figure 6-9) could then be further subdivided with "**Wind_Speed < 10**" as shown in Figure 6-10. With this step, the bottom row of left side of Figure 6-9 becomes the left (Yes) branch and the top two rows become the right (No) branch.

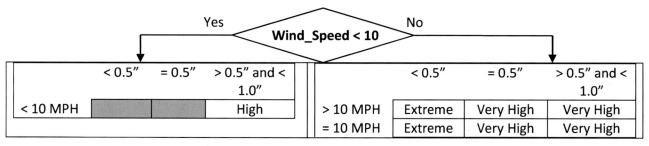

Figure 6-10: Second Selection to Implement the Fire Danger Decision Table

From there, the left side can be distinguished by "**Rainfall <= 0.5**" and the right side with "**Rainfall < 0.5**". With these decisions, we are down to specific fire danger ratings that we can act upon.

We would do a similar process on the right side of the original "**Rainfall < 1.0**" selection to complete the construct. We could simply report **"Unspecified"** for the red entry cases where no rating was specified. Likewise, we could report **"Conflict"** for the two yellow entries where there was conflicting direction given. Ideally, we would go back to the author of the specification and use our decision table to point out the problems and ask them for an appropriate resolution.

The resulting RAPTOR flowchart for this problem is shown in the three snippets of flowcharts provided as Figures 6-11, 6-12, and 6-13. Figure 6-11 shows the top level organization of the resulting flowchart. Here we have "collapsed" the two lower level Selection constructs (by clicking the box next to the decision diamond).

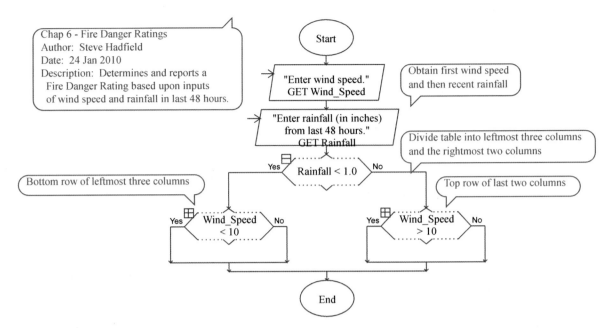

Figure 6-11: Top-Level Flowchart for the Fire Danger Flowchart

The left (Yes) branch starting with the "**Wind_Speed < 10**" decision expression is shown in Figure 6-12.

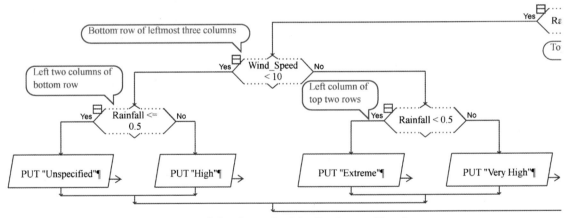

Figure 6-12: Left (Yes) Branch of the Fire Danger Flowchart

The right (Yes) branch of the nested selection starting with the "Wind_Speed > 10" decision expression is shown in Figure 6-13. Take a few minutes to match these nested Selection constructions to the Decision Table decomposition from earlier.

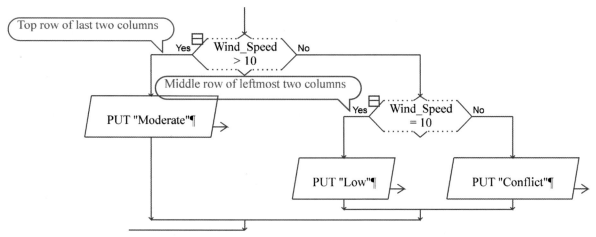

Figure 6-13: Right (No) Branch of the Fire Danger Flowchart

With the flowchart created, the Test step will verify that it correctly handles each of the 15 different types of inputs corresponding to entries in the decision table. The decision table (Table 6-) includes the addition of test input values to define the 15 needed test cases.

Table 6-3: Fire Danger Decision Table with Test Case Input Values

		Rainfall in Last 48 Hours				
		< 0.5"	= 0.5"	> 0.5" and < 1.0"	=1.0"	> 1.0"
Wind	> 10 MPH	15, 0.0	15, 0.5	15, 0.7	15, 1.0	15, 2.0
Speed	= 10 MPH	10, 0.0	10, 0.5	10, 0.7	10, 1.0	10, 2.0
	< 10 MPH	5, 0.0	5, 0.5	5, 0.7	5, 1.0	5, 2.0

Conclusion

In this chapter, we have explored several methods and tools for analyzing and understanding the requirements of a problem so that we can more efficiently and effectively address and resolve the issues. The first method we learned about had us **Extract Key Points** from the problem statement and categorize them as inputs, processing steps, outputs, and variables. We then **Asked Probing Questions** to fill in gaps left from the problem statements. Then we made detailed **List of Tasks with Variables** that are needed for our algorithm development.

To better understand and communicate the user interface for graphical algorithms, we learned about the use of **Pictures and Sketches** as well as **Storyboards** to animate the interactions with the graphics.

Finally, we studied the use of **Decision Tables** to help us analyze complex decision conditions and then develop appropriate combinations of Selection constructs to implement the needed decision making.

Exercises

1. Create a List of Tasks for making a sandwich that a robot could follow. Remember, a robot is just a special computer, so make your tasks very specific.

2. Draw a series of storyboards for your favorite card game like they're going to be played using computer graphics. If you can't think of any, try Go Fish!

3. The National Weather Service uses a variety of criteria to declare various types of winter storm advisories and warnings. The narrative below is a simplified and hypothetical requirements statement for winter storm advisories and warnings based upon snowfall rate and wind speed (with contradiction and omissions purposefully included). Analyze this requirements statement using an appropriate decision table. Then write a RAPTOR algorithm that first accepts a snowfall rate and then a wind speed. The algorithm should then report the appropriate winter weather advisory / warning or "ERROR - Contradiction" if more than one output was specified or "ERROR – Unspecified Situation" if no, direction was provided.

> If the snowfall rate is 4 inches per hour or higher, report "WSW" for Winter Storm Warning. If the snowfall rate is 1 inch per hour or more but less than 4 inches per hour and the wind speed is less than 35 miles per hour, report "WSA" for Winter Storm Advisory. If the wind speed is at least 35 miles per hour and the snow fall rate is at least 1 inch per hour, report "BW" for Blizzard Warning. If the snowfall rate is greater than zero inches per hour and the wind speed is less than 15 miles per hour, report "S" for Snow.

4. Wet Bulb Globe Temperature (WBGT) is an outdoor activity warning system based upon temperature and humidity. The narrative requirements statement below provides a grossly over-simplified version of WBGT category determination. Analyze this requirements statement using an appropriate decision table. Then write a RAPTOR algorithm based upon this specification that first accepts temperature and then humidity. The algorithm outputs the color-based condition per the specification. If no category has been specified for a given set of input, report "ERROR – Unspecified". If conflicting direction has been given for the inputs, report "ERROR – Conflict".

> If the temperature is 70 or below and the humidity is less than 75%, report "White". If the temperature is 70 or below and the humidity is 75% or more, report "Green". If the humidity is greater than 75% and the temperature is 90 degrees of more, report "Black". If the temperature is more than 70 degrees but less than or equal to 90 degrees and the humidity is 25% or less, report "Green". If the temperature is more than 90 degrees and the humidity is 25% or less, report "Yellow". Also, report "Yellow" if the temperature is 90 degrees or less but more than 70 degrees and the humidity is more than 25% but less than or equal to 75%. Report "Red" if the temperature is 90 degrees or more and the humidity is more than 25%, but less than or equal to 75%.

7. Sub-Charts: Breaking Algorithms into Manageable Pieces

In Chapter 3, we learned about RAPTOR Graphics and used the many built-in procedures and functions to draw in and interact with the graphic window in RAPTOR. In this chapter, we will create our own special type of procedures called **Subcharts** and then call them much like we called the built-in graphics procedures earlier on. Subcharts provide us a very useful means to break a big algorithm into meaningful pieces, just as we broke a big problem down into a series of small manageable problems in the previous chapter. In fact, the decomposition of our problem into a series of smaller problems maps directly to our use of subcharts to solve those smaller problems.

Functional Decomposition

In the Order Pricing problem of the previous chapter, we addressed the following problem statement:

> **Write an algorithm to obtain product orders from customers and price the orders for the customers. The pricing shall apply bulk purchase discounts and state tax rates. The algorithm needs to provide the user with an echo of their inputs together with the discount, tax, and total price.**

First, we extracted key points from the problem statement and created a table identifying inputs, processing, outputs, and variables. Next, we asked some probing questions to identify relevant details that were missing from the original description of the problem (the Understand step). Next, we moved to the Design step and made a list of tasks and broke them down into additional sub-tasks where needed using a technique called Functional Decomposition. This effort resulted in the List of Tasks below which we could implement as a single RAPTOR flowchart. However, this flowchart would be very long and complicated. In Figure 7-1, we see the structure of a flowchart for this example and notice that it includes 35 symbols!

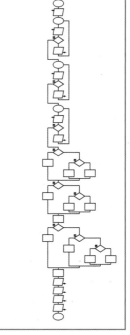

Figure 7-1: Single Flowchart Version of the Order Pricing Example

List of Tasks for the Order Pricing Example:

- Obtain the product order information
  - Input customer name
  - Input customer's state
    - Check that customer's state is either CO, WY, UT, or NM
  - Input product type
    - Check that a valid product type was entered
  - Input quantity ordered
- Calculate the order price
  - Look up price of the product type
    - If product is snow skis, then product price is $300
    - If product is snowboard, then product price is $200
    - If product is snowshoes, then product price is $100
  - Determine the discount based upon the quantity ordered
    - If quantity is 6 to 10, then discount is 10%
    - If quantity ordered is 11 or more, then discount is 20%

- o Calculate the order price as (product_price * quantity) * (1-discount)
- o Determine sales tax based upon state and order price as (order_price * tax_rate)
  - If state is CO, then tax rate is 7%
  - If state is WY, then tax rate is 5%
  - If state is UT, then tax rate is 4%
  - If state is NM, then tax rate is 5.5%
- o Calculate total price of the order as (order_price + sales_tax)
- Report the order pricing information
  - o Report order information
    - Output customer's name and state, product type, and quantity ordered
  - o Report discount
  - o Report tax
  - o Report total price

RAPTOR provides the Subchart feature as a means to break such complicated flowcharts into smaller parts that exist as distinct tabs and can be run via the Call symbol. The screenshot in Figure 7-2 shows an alternative form of our Order Pricing algorithm that makes extensive use of subcharts (which are shown as tabs within the Workspace area).

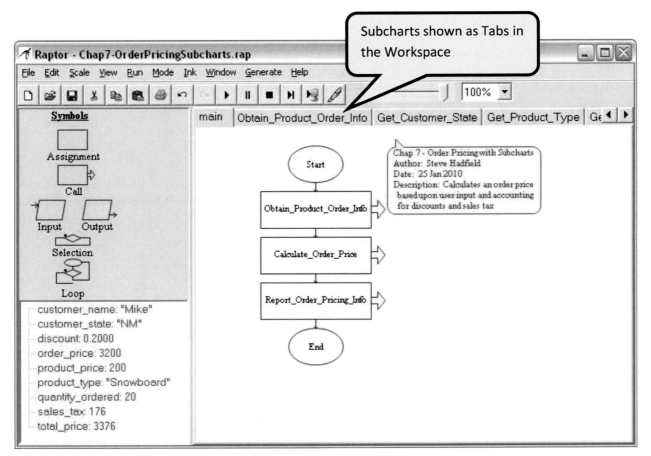

Figure 7-2: Order Pricing RAPTOR Algorithm Using Subcharts

Creating and Using Subcharts

RAPTOR gives us two ways to create subcharts:

1. Right click on an existing subchart (such as Main) and select "Add Subchart" from the resulting menu.
2. Insert a Call symbol and specify a new name for a subchart. RAPTOR will realize that it does not exist and ask if you would like to create a subchart with that name.

Also of note is that RAPTOR subcharts do not allow for parameters (values passed to it like in "**Draw_Circle(50, 100, 25, Red, Filled)**"). Rather we just have the name of the subchart with no parameters. However, we can access all our variables across subcharts which allows the Main subchart and other subcharts to share information with one another. Later we will learn about RAPTOR **Procedures** which do allow us to include parameters.

The challenge with sharing variables across subcharts is to keep track of when and how updates to the variables' values are made. Problems can arise if a variable's value is updated in an unexpected way. For example, in the flowchart of Figure 7-3, the **Draw_Circle(X_Loc, Y_Loc, 10, Blue, Filled)** may be expecting the values of 150 and 200 to be in **X_Loc** and **Y_Loc**, respectively. However, if the **Do_Something** subchart changes those values, the subsequent call to Draw_Circle would have the circle drawn in a different location. Such a problem would be hard to find as its cause is hidden in the separate subchart named **Do_Something**.

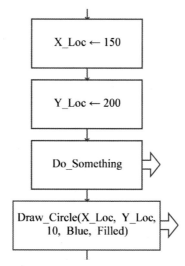

Figure 7-3: Dangers of Sharing Variables

Getting back to our Order Pricing example, we see from the List of Tasks that there are three top level tasks shown as the leftmost bullets. We could create a separate subchart for each one of these which gives us the very simple and elegant Main subchart shown in Figure 7-4. Notice how we use very descriptive names for the subcharts that describe exactly what is being done in that subchart.

Another relevant issue deals with the size of each subchart; that is, how many symbols it contains. A reasonable 'rule of thumb' would be to have no more than 10 to 20 symbols on a subchart.

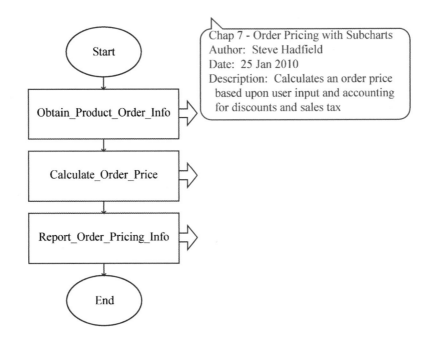

Figure 7-4: Main Subchart for New Order Pricing Algorithm

The next thing that we would do is create the flowchart for the first subchart which is **Obtain_Product_Order_Info**. In particular, we will address each of the sub-bullets under the first primary bullet in our List of Tasks.

- Obtain the product order information
  - Input customer name
  - Input customer's state
    - Check that customer's state is either CO, WY, UT, or NM
  - Input product type
    - Check that a valid product type was entered
  - Input quantity ordered

 Some of these sub-bullets are bigger jobs and should likely be implemented with their own subcharts. **Get_Customer_State**, **Get_Product_Type**, and **Get_Quantity_Ordered** could all be implemented by separate subcharts as they require validation of the user's input. The **Obtain_Product_Order_Info** subchart is shown in Figure 7-5.

80

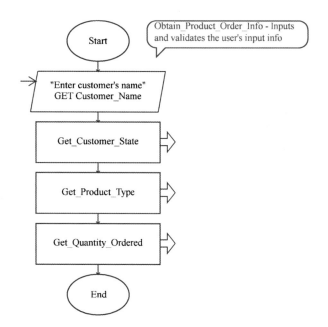

Figure 7-5: Obtain_Product_Order_Info Subchart

The additional subcharts called from **Obtain_Product_Order_Info** are shown and described in Figures 7-6, 7-7, and 7-8. Note that they follow the Input Validation Loop format that we learned earlier in Chapter 5. In the **Get_Customer_State** subchart, the loop exit condition first checks that the value entered for the **Customer_State** variable is a string and then it checks for one of the four appropriate state identifiers. If we did not do the **Is_String()** check, the user could enter a number for **Customer_State** and it would cause our flowchart to crash. Similar checks are done in the input validation loops of the other subcharts.

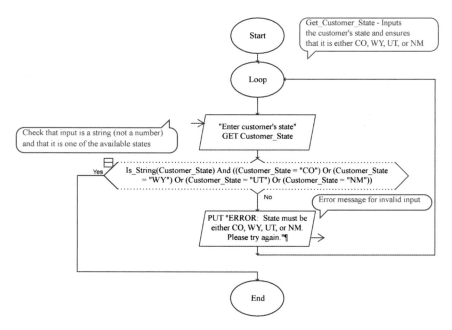

Figure 7-6: Get_Customer_State Subchart

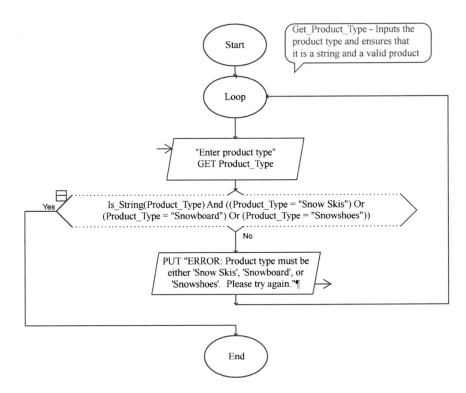

Figure 7-7: Get_Product_Type Subchart

The **Get_Quantity_Ordered** subchart obtains a number from the user and thus we use **Is_Number()** in our check.

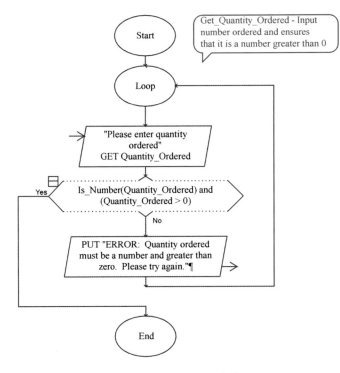

Figure 7-8: Get_Quantity_Ordered Subchart

By breaking our flowchart into a series of subcharts, each part is very easy to understand and implement. This is a great problem solving technique called **Functional Decomposition**. The one piece that is missing is a road map of which subcharts call which other subcharts. The diagram in Figure 7-9 is called a **Structure Chart**. A Structure Chart provides this road map showing all of the subcharts and which ones call which other ones.

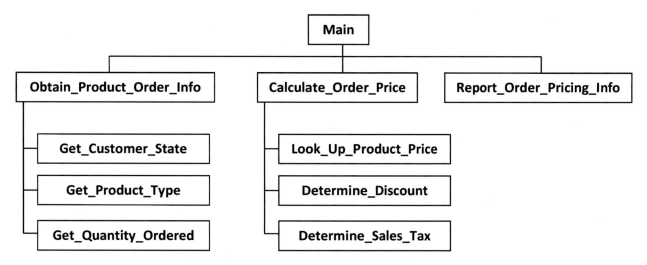

Figure 7-9: Structure Chart for the Order Pricing Algorithm

The remaining subcharts for the Order Pricing example are shown in Figures 7-10 through 7-14.

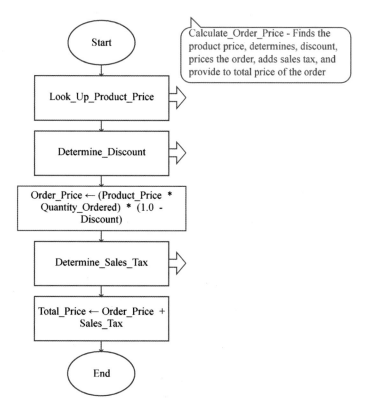

Figure 7-10: Calculate_Order_Price Subchart

Note that in the **Look_Up_Product_Price** subchart (Figure 7-11), we do not have to explicitly check for **Product_Type = "Snowshoes"**. We were careful to validate the value for Product_Type when it was input so we know that if it does not equal "Snow Skis" or "Snowboard", then it must be "Snowshoes".

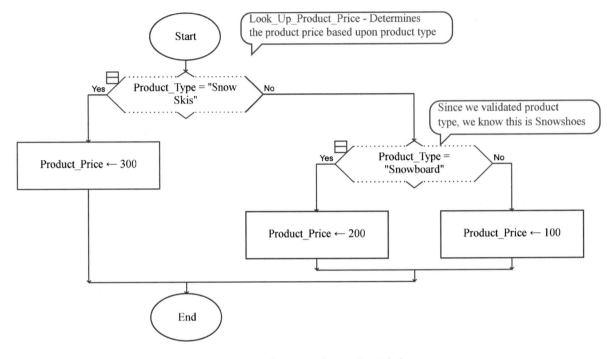

Figure 7-11: Look_Up_Product_Price Subchart

The **Determine_Discount** subchart (Figure 7-12) uses a Cascading Selection as discussed in Chapter 4.

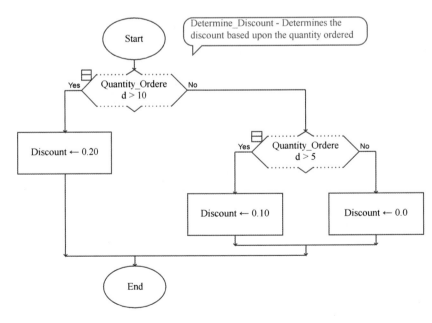

Figure 7-12: Determine_Discount Subchart

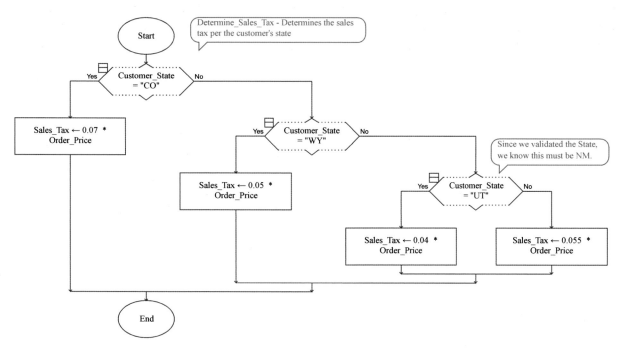

Figure 7-13: Determine_Sales_Tax Subchart

The last subchart, **Report_Order_Pricing_Info**, simply outputs the final results (Figure 7-14). Comparing these subcharts to the portion of the List of Tasks that they implement, we see that there is a direct correspondence and can readily see how these smaller flowcharts follow from the listed tasks. We see that the List of Tasks is very helpful in the development of our entire algorithm. Also of great use was the List of Variables as it helped to ensure that we always named the variables correctly.

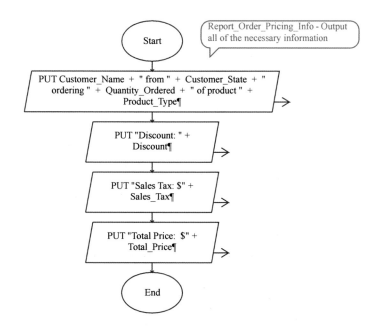

Figure 7-14: Report_Order_Pricing_Info Subchart

85

Conclusion

Between the previous chapter and this current one, we saw how to refine a problem statement first into a list of high-level tasks and then repeatedly focus on the individual high-level tasks to further define the lower level tasks needed to accomplish each. The functional decomposition problem solving approach proved very useful in breaking up a complex algorithm into a series of very manageable pieces. We then saw how those pieces could be easily implemented with RAPTOR subcharts. In the next chapter, we'll further explore functional decomposition and the use of subcharts as we learn how to animate our graphics.

Exercises

1. Modify the first Example Problem in Chapter 3 (shipping water skis) to use sub-charts.

2. Modify the second Example Problem in Chapter 3 (revealing the circles) to use sub-charts.

3. Write a RAPTOR algorithm that moves a ball around in a graphics window. At first, the ball should bounce off of the walls of the graphics window. When the user presses any key, the ball should 'wrap' around the window; that is, if the ball touches the right wall, it should move to appear on the left wall and, if it crosses the top wall, it should appear on the bottom wall. When the user hits a key again, the ball should go back to its bouncing behavior. Hitting subsequent keys should continually 'toggle' the ball between the two different behaviors until the user left-clicks the mouse which should end the program and get rid of the graphics window. Use separate sub-charts for each of the two different behaviors.

4. Reaccomplish Challenge Exercise from Chapter 2 (repeated below), using functional decomposition and sub-charts. Recommend you have sub-charts for (1) getting a lat-long that does the degrees-minutes-seconds-direction to single signed angle in radians, (2) calling (1) four times to get the latitudes and longitudes for the two points, and (3) to do the Haversine formula calculation.

CHALLENGE EXERCISE: The distance between two points on the surface of the Earth can be calculated based on the Great Circle distance using the Haversine formula. Write an algorithm that accepts two locations expressed as latitudes and longitudes each given in terms of degrees, minutes, seconds, and direction (N, S, E, W). Convert the degrees, minutes, and seconds into a single angle value as follows:

$$angle\_in\_degrees = degrees + \frac{minutes}{60} + \frac{seconds}{3600}$$

Convert each *angle_in_degrees* into radians as follows:

$$angle\_in\_radians = angle\_in\_degre \quad * \frac{\pi}{180}$$

For West longitudes and South latitudes, make the angles negative.

Calculate the Haversine formula in the following three parts:

$$a = \sin^2\left(\frac{lat2 - lat1}{2}\right) + \left(\cos(lat1) * \cos(lat2) * \sin^2\left(\frac{long2 - long1}{2}\right)\right)$$

$$c = 2 * arctan\left(\sqrt{a}, \sqrt{(1-a)}\right)$$

$$distance = R * c$$

where R is the average radius of the Earth (6,371km or 3959 miles) and the two points on the earth are $(lat1, long1)$ and $(lat2, long2)$ where these latitudes and longitudes have been converted to single values in radians. Reference: https://www.movable-type.co.uk/scripts/latlong.html.

8. Animations: Making Graphics Move

Making graphics move and react to user inputs can make for interesting and engaging algorithms. In this chapter, we will learn two approaches to animating graphics: **(1) Erase object – Move object – Draw object** and **(2) Erase scene – Move object – Draw scene**. We will also use a buffered image to smooth out the movement of the graphics. Functional decomposition and RAPTOR's subcharts will help to keep the complexity of the algorithms manageable.

Creating Animations

For our first animation, we will bounce a ball around in a graphics window using the **Erase object – Move object – Draw object** approach. The **Main** flow chart for the bouncing ball animation is shown below. The **Initialize_Animation** subchart provides all of the setup actions for the animation and is shown separately on the next page. The Loop construct keeps the animation moving until the left mouse button is pressed. The call to **Mouse_Button_Pressed** checks if it is time to exit the loop. Within the loop, there is a call to the built-in **Delay_For()** procedure to keep the animation moving at a reasonable speed. The ball is erased in its current location by drawing it using the background color. The Move_Ball subchart updates the location of the ball and is shown two pages forward. The ball is then drawn again in its new position. Prior to completion, we call the built-in **Close_Graphics_Window** to compete the program.

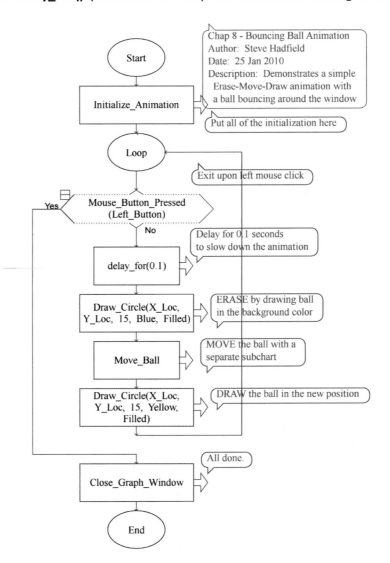

Figure 8-1: Sample Bouncing Ball Animation Flowchart

88

The **Initialize_Animation** subchart (in Figure 8-2) contains all the actions needed to set up the animation. First, it opens the graphics window and then sets the window title to include some instructions to the user. The graphics window is then cleared and colored blue. The initial X and Y locations of the ball are randomly generated using the **Floor()** and **Random** function calls in a formula such as the one below:

$$\text{Floor}(380 * \text{Random} + 10)$$

The **Random** function returns a randomly generated number starting at zero up to (but not including) one, shown [0, 1) in mathematical notation[6]. We multiply this value times a number such as 380 to get a random number in the range [0, 380) and then add an offset, such as 10 to get the number into the range of [10, 390) which falls nicely with the screen width of 400. Finally, the **Floor()** function trims off any decimal part. We use a similar formula to establish the movement of the ball in the X and Y directions using the **X_Change** and **Y_Change** variables. These values will be later added to the **X_Loc** and **Y_Loc** location variables to move the ball. Note that both **X_Change** and **Y_Change** take on values in the range of [-15, 14].

The small screenshot in Figure 8-3 shows the bouncing ball animation in action.

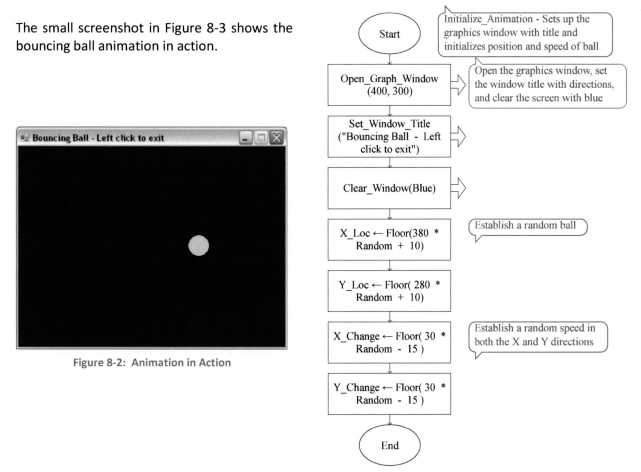

Figure 8-2: Animation in Action

Figure 8-3: Initialize_Animation Subchart

---

[6] In mathematical notation, a square bracket "[" or "]" means that endpoint is included; whereas parenthesis "(" or ")" mean everything up to, but not including, the endpoint is in the interval.

The **Move_Ball** subchart (Figure 8-4) implements the movement of the ball. The **X_Loc** location is updated by adding **X_Change** to it. Note **X_Change** could be negative or positive moving the ball left or right accordingly. Then the updated **X_Loc** value is checked for being up against either the left or right sides of the graphics window. If **X_Loc** is within 10 pixels of either side, the **X_Change** variable is negated (multiplied by -1) to reverse the ball's X direction for the next update. A similar update and check is done for the **Y_Loc** location.

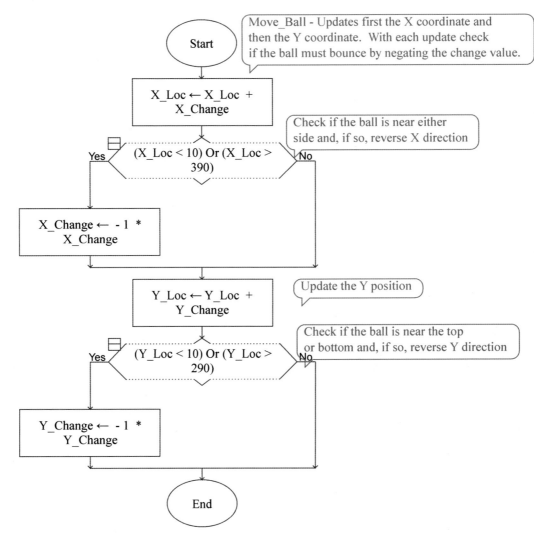

Figure 8-4: Move_Ball Subchart

The **Erase object – Move object – Draw object** approach works because the background is always just blue. However, it would not work with a more complicated background as we would need to know what to redraw after erasing the ball's old location. Our next example will illustrate this and show us the alternative **Erase scene – Move object – Draw scene** approach.

Moving a Complex Object on a Complex Scene

The objective of the next animation is to move a more complicated object across a more complex scene. In particular, we'll move our UFO (from Chapter 3) around a nice mountain scene until the left mouse button is clicked. A screenshot of our algorithm in action is shown in Figure 8-5.

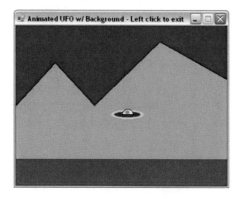

Figure 8-5: Animated UFO with Background Algorithm in Action

The Main subchart for our animated UFO algorithm is shown in Figure 8-6. Note that it includes similar subcharts to initialize the animation and update the location of the UFO as our bouncing ball example. However, the algorithm also uses three new built-in procedures: **Freeze_Graph_Window**, **Update_Graph_Window**, and **Unfreeze_Graph_Window**.

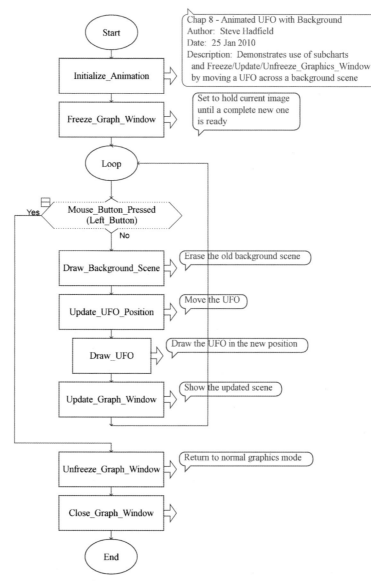

Figure 8-6: Animated UFO with Background Main Subchart

The call to **Freeze_Graph_Window** causes all subsequent updates to the graphics window to be made to a hidden copy, called a buffer. The call to **Update_Graph_Window** displays this hidden graphics window revealing the updates. Additional updates, after the call to **Update_Graph_Window**, are again hidden until **Update_Graph_Window** is once again called. The effect produced provides a very smooth animation. The buffered (and hidden) image approach to graphics is turned off by the call to

Unfreeze_Graph_Window. Note that it is important to only call **Update_Graph_Window** after the entire new scene has been drawn.

The **Initialize_Animation** subchart is shown in Figure 8-7 and very much resembles the corresponding subchart from our bouncing ball example.

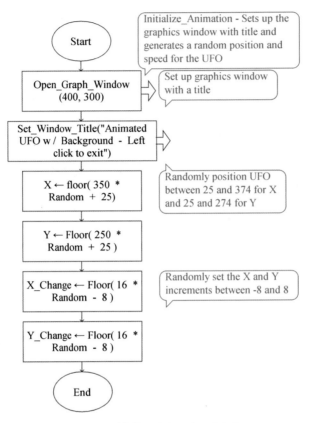

Figure 8-7: Initialize_Animation Subchart

The **Update_UFO_Position** subchart is also shown in Figure 8-8 and closely resembles the **Move_Ball** subchart from the previous example. The X and Y positions of the UFO are each updated and then checked to see if the UFO's position is near a boundary and needs to be 'bounced' by reversing a direction.

The remaining two subcharts are **Draw_UFO** and **Draw_Background_Scene**. They are shown in Figures 8-9 and 8-10, respectively.

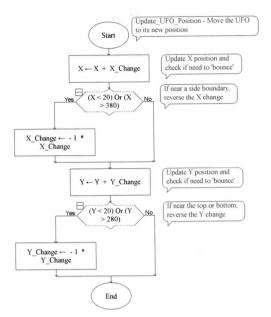

Figure 8-8: Update_UFO_Position Subchart

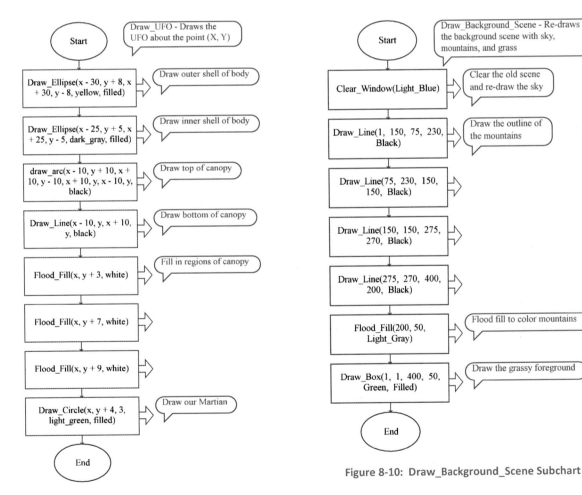

Figure 8-9: Draw_UFO Subchart

Figure 8-10: Draw_Background_Scene Subchart

Adding Sounds

RAPTOR also allows us to add sounds to our algorithms. The three built-in procedures that do this are described below and can be run via a Call symbol.

Built-In Sound Procedure	Description
Play_Sound(filename)	Plays the sound file specified by filename one time and pauses execution of the algorithm while it does so.
Play_Sound_Background(filename)	Plays the sound file specified by filename one time but does not pause execution of the algorithm while it does so.
Play_Sound_Background_Loop(filename)	Continuously plays the sound file specified by filename while not pausing execution of the algorithm.

More details on graphics, animations, and sounds can be found in RAPTOR's General Help facility.

Adding Images

To really enhance our graphics, we can load in images in a variety of formats and the display them in your graphics window to include moving them around the screen. First you need to use an assignment symbol to call **Load_Bitmap()** function and assign the results to a variable for future use. See how this is done in Figure 8-11. Images can be either Bitmap (.bmp), JPEG (.jpg), or GIF (.gif).

Once an image has been loaded into a variable, as in Figure 8-11, we can use the **Draw_Bitmap** to display the image in the graphics window much as we would use **Draw_Box** specifying opposite corners. Figure 8-12 demonstrates how **Draw_Bitmap** could be called.

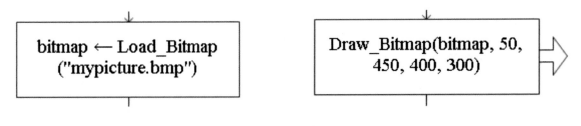

Figure 8-11: Load_Bitmap Example   Figure 8-12: Draw_Bitmap Example

Conclusion

Within this chapter, we have learned how to animate computer graphics using two different methods. In the first method, we erased the moving object, moved it to its new location, and then re-drew it there. This worked fine as long it was easy to erase just the object. However, when the object was placed on a complicated scene, the second method of redrawing the scene, moving the object, and re-drawing the object on the fresh scene worked better.

In addition, we used a buffering scheme to draw the next frame of the animation in the background and then show it all at once to smooth out the animation and avoid flickering of the image. The buffering scheme as turned on with a call to **Freeze_Graph_Window** and the updated frames displayed with **Update_Graph_Window**.

Exercises

1. Modify the bouncing ball example to bounce something else, like a square or a triangle.

2. Modify our UFO animation to add a second UFO and make this UFO bounce off the left and right sides of the screen like the bouncing ball.

3. Write a RAPTOR algorithm that bounces two balls around the graphics window. When the balls collide, change both the color of the balls and the background color randomly. End the program with the user clicks the left mouse button. The two balls will collide when the distance between their center points is less than the sum of their radii.

4. Enhance your Exercise 3 algorithm so that the animation stops when the user hits a key and then resumes when they hit the key again; that is, hitting a key acts as an on/off toggle.

5. **CHALLENGE EXERCISE**: Create an animated version of the classic Pong game. Reference: http://www.ponggame.org/.

9. Arrays: Dealing with Groups of Related Data

The Counted Loop in Chapter 5 provided a wonderful means to obtain and process a set of many related values such as test scores or business expenses. By dealing with one of the data elements at a time, we could easily total the values, find their average, or determine their maximum or minimum. With all of these, we only needed a single variable for the input values as we dealt with them one at a time and re-used that variable for the next value.

However, we frequently encounter problems that require us to retain all of the values as we will have to use them at different times and for different purposes. For example, if we wanted to list all of the test scores that were above the average, we would need to:

- Read in the test scores
- Calculate the average by dividing the total of the scores by how many there are
- Go back through the test scores comparing each one to the average and reporting it if it is above the average

Note that we cannot do the third step until the prior two steps are complete. Therefore we must store all of the scores to use in the final step (else we would have to ask for them again).

What is an Array?

The mechanism for storing a group of related data is called an **Array Variable**. The array variable has a single name that references all of the elements and then uses an index number to access individual members of the group. For example, Scores[5] would access the 5th score in an array called "Scores".

So our formal definition of an Array Variable is:

> An <u>Array Variable</u> is a collection of variables, each storing a single value, where the collection has one base name and individual variables in the collection are identified with a unique index value.

Consider the diagram of the Scores array below. The Array Name is Scores. The Array Index values go from 1 to 5 and provide access to the five elements of the array. The five scores are 90, 85, 70, 93, and 87 and they are accessed as Scores[1], Scores[2], Scores[3], Scores[4], and Scores[5], respectively.

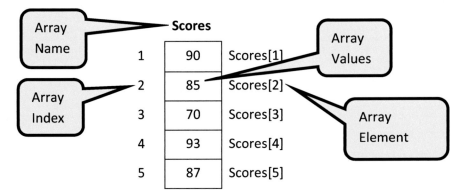

Figure 9-1: Description of the Scores Array

When we access the 5th score in the array as "Scores[5]", the array name is "Scores", the index is "5" (the 5 is held within square brackets to identify it as the index), and the value in that element of the array is "87".

Metaphorically, we could think of the array as a group of post office boxes. The index would then be the post office (PO) box number. The value in the array would be the letter contained in that PO box. Note that if the PO box was an array, it would only be able to hold one letter at a time.

Importantly, the index does not need to be an explicit number (such as "5" in the case above). The index can be a variable that holds a number. For example, we could set a variable named "Index" to 5 and then reference "Scores[Index]" to get at the value of 87 in the example above.

Using a variable for the index into an array allows us to do things like use a Counted Loop to go through all the elements of an array by using the loop index as an index into the array. Consider the **Find_Position_Of_Value** subchart in Figure 9-2. It uses the standard **ITEM** (**I**nitialize-**T**est-**E**valuate-**M**odify) counted loop to go through all of the values in the **Values** array looking for a user-specified target value. The variable "**i**" is used as both the loop index and the index into the array. Note, another subchart (which we will see later) was used to fill the array with values.

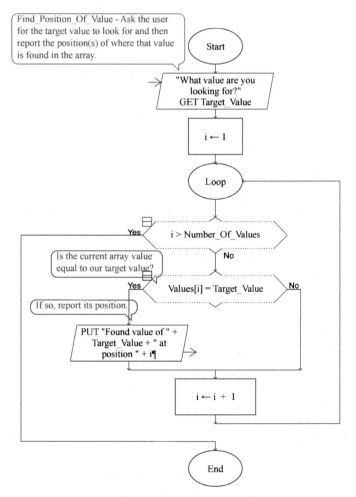

Figure 9-2: Find_Position_Of_Value Subchart

Putting Values into an Array

Before we can do things with the values in an array, we need to put the values into the array. We do this in a manner very similar to other variables -- typically using either Input or Assignment symbols. The **Get_Values** subchart (Figure 9-3) asks the user for how many values there are and then uses a counted ITEM loop to input each value (one-at-a-time) into the array elements. Again, the loop index **i** is also used to index into the array called **Values**.

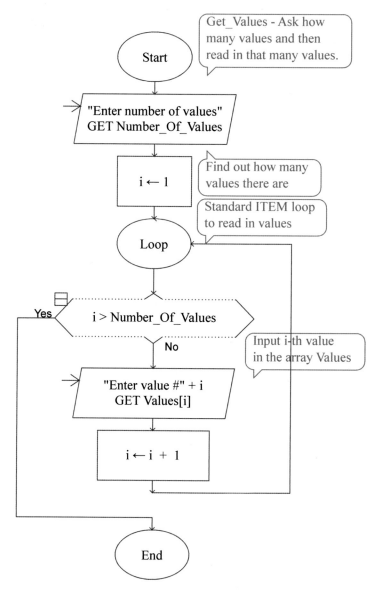

Figure 9-3: Get_Values Subchart

A very nice feature of RAPTOR is that we do not need to know the number of array values up front; RAPTOR will create additional elements in our arrays as values are provided to them. Furthermore, we can create and initialize a number of array elements all at one time. The Assignment

98

Values[100] ← 5

will not only set the 100th entry in the Values array to 5, but also create entries 1 through 99, setting them to zero.

To consider another example of the need to use arrays, we will report all the values that are above the average. To do this, we must first determine the average. The **Find_Average** subchart (Figure 9-4) does this for us. It uses the Total variable to sum up each of the values in the array, adding the next value from the array to its running sum each time through the loop. After exiting the loop, the Total is divided by the number of values in the array to attain the average. Note, the array has already been filled prior to this subchart being called.

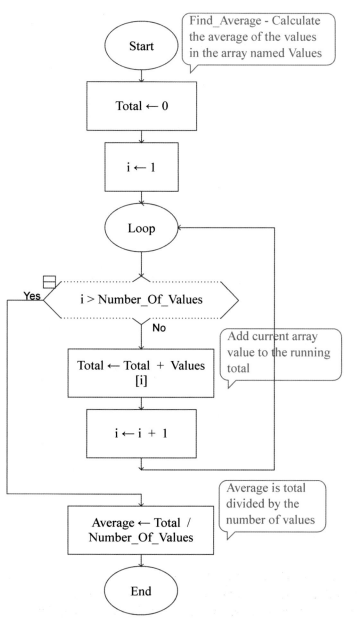

Figure 9-4: Find_Average Subchart

Once the average has been calculated, we can go through the array one more time comparing each value in the array to the average and reporting both the value and position within the array for each value that is over the average. The **Report_Those_Above_Average** subchart below accomplishes this for us.

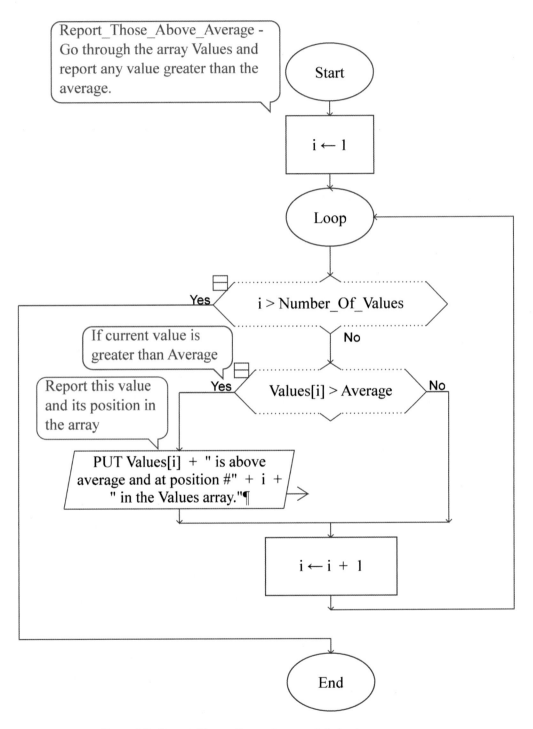

Figure 9-5: Report_Those_Above_Average Subchart

Now that we are starting to get feel for array variables and their usage, let us practice our algorithmic reasoning and functional decomposition skills with a problem that requires the use of arrays.

Problem Statement:

> **Read in a number of corporate salaries and report those that are within $10,000 of the maximum salary.**

Extracting key points from this problem statement, we come up with the inputs, processing, outputs, and variables shown in Table 9-1:

Table 9-1: Initial Input-Process-Output with Variables

Inputs	Processing	Outputs	Variables
• Salaries	• Input Salaries • Report Salaries within $10,000 of maximum	• Salaries within $10,000 of maximum	• Salaries

Next we start to ask some probing questions such as:
- How many salaries will be provided?
- How will we know what the maximum salary is?

We learn that salaries will be provided one at a time until a value of -1 is provided as a marker that there are no more salaries. We surmise that we will need to read in the salaries until this marker is input and also count how many salaries are entered as we go.

We also find out that we will have to determine the maximum salary ourselves and that the user also wants to know which salary was the largest (a new requirement found when "Asking Probing Questions"!). Our table of inputs, processing tasks, outputs and variables expands to become what is shown in Table 9-2 (note that additions have been highlighted):

Table 9-2: Updated Input-Process-Output with Variables

Inputs	Processing	Outputs	Variables
• Salaries	• Input Salaries • Count number of Salaries • Determine maximum salary and its position • Report maximum salary and its position • Report Salaries within $10,000 of maximum	• Maximum Salary and its position • Salaries within $10,000 of maximum	• Salaries • Number of Salaries • Maximum Salary • Position of Maximum Salary

This table, the culmination of the Understand step, provides us an excellent guide for developing both a List of Tasks and a List of Variables for this problem.

Our initial list of top level tasks is:

- Input Salaries
- Determine count of salaries
- Determine position of maximum salary (if we have the position, we also easily have the value)
- Report value and position of maximum salary
- Report salaries within $10,000 of maximum

Using functional decomposition, we then consider each top level task individually and break them down into additional detailed tasks as needed. The resulting full List of Tasks then becomes:

- Input Salaries
    - Repeatedly input in salary values
    - If input is a -1, exit loop
    - Else store the salary in the next array entry
- Determine count of salaries
- Determine position of maximum salary (if we have the position, we also easily have the value)
    - Assume the maximum salary is the first salary
    - Repeatedly compare each salary to the current maximum
    - If the current salary is greater, record it as the new maximum salary
- Report value and position of maximum salary
- Report salaries within $10,000 of maximum
    - Repeatedly access each salary
    - If it is within $10,000 of the maximum salary, report it

Our **List of Variables** is:

Salaries (an array)   **Number_Of_Salaries**   **Position_Of_Max_Salary**

Note that we do not need a separate variable for the maximum salary since we know the position of the maximum salary and can use it to get the maximum salary by:

Salaries[Position_Of_Max_Salary]

To implement this algorithm, we could start with the Main flowchart in Figure 9-6 which implements our top level of our List of Tasks. Note we have two symbols in the Main subchart for reporting the result of our algorithm, one a normal output and one a subchart performing multiple outputs.

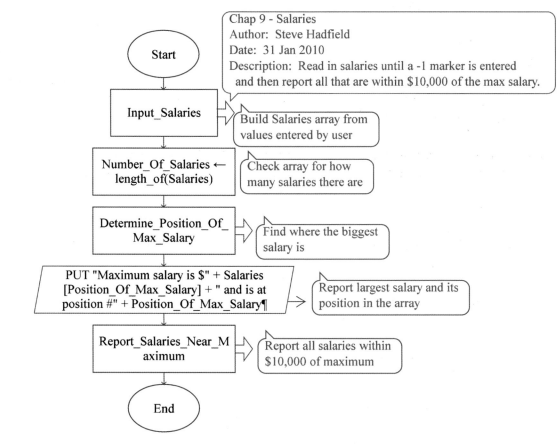

Figure 9-6: Salaries Algorithm's Main Subchart

In the Main subchart above, we use the Length_Of() function to return the number of entries in the array, which is how many salaries there are. We could also just call this function each time we needed the value instead of using the variable Number_Of_Salaries.

Three of the top level list of tasks are more complicated and are implemented on their own subcharts. The **Input_Salaries** subchart (Figure 9-7) uses **i** as both a counter of how many salaries have been entered and as an index into the Salaries array. Before the loop exit condition, there is an Input symbol to get the next input from the user. If the input is the end of input marker, -1, then the loop exits. Otherwise, the number of salaries is incremented and this latest salary input is copied into the array's next location.

103

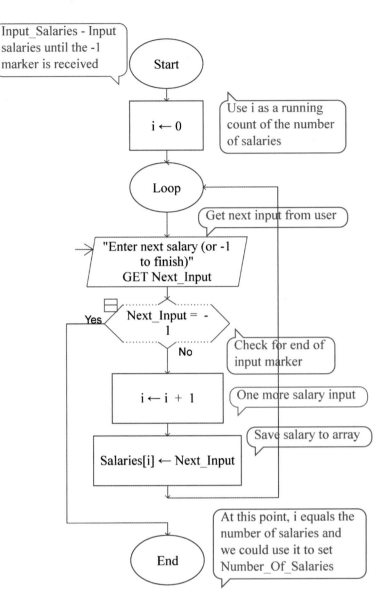

Figure 9-7: Input_Salaries Subchart

The next subchart is called **Determine_Position_Of_Max_Salary** (see Figure 9-8). This flowchart sets the initial value of **Position_Of_Max_Salary** to 1 assuming that the first salary is our current largest. The algorithm then goes through each of the salaries in the array and compares the current salary to this last known largest salary. If the current salary is larger, **Position_Of_Max_Salary** is set to the position of this current salary (held in the loop index variable **i**). When the loop exits, **Position_Of_Max_Salary** will store the index of where the largest salary occurs in the array.

An interesting question to ask is "What happens when the maximum salary occurs more than once?" In this case, our current **Determine_Position_Of_Max_Salary** subchart will set **Position_Of_Max_Salary** to the first occurrence of the largest salary. Can you see why this is?

If the Selection condition was changed to:

Salaries[i] >= Salaries[Position_Of_Max_Salary]

which instance of the largest salary would be saved in **Position_Of_Max_Salary**?

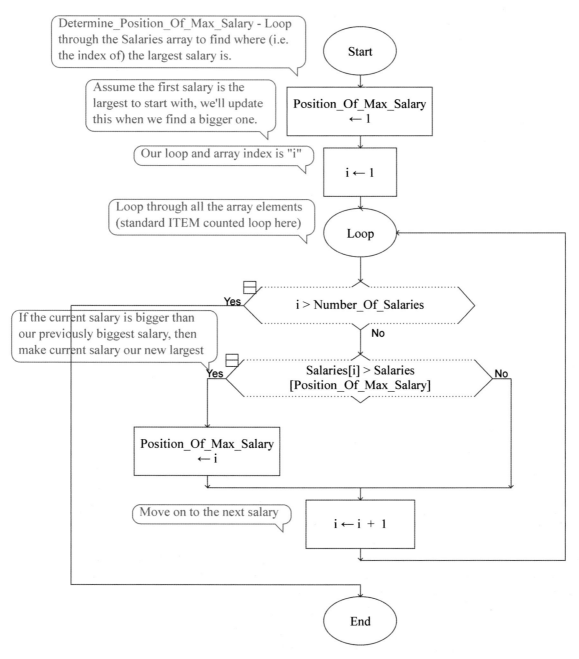

Figure 9-8: Determine_Position_Of_Max_Salary Subchart

In our final subchart, **Report_Salaries_Near_Maximum** (shown in Figure 9-9), a standard ITEM counted loop is used to go through all of the salaries in the array and check them for being greater than or equal to the maximum salary - $10,000. Those that pass this test are reported with their position in the **Salaries** array.

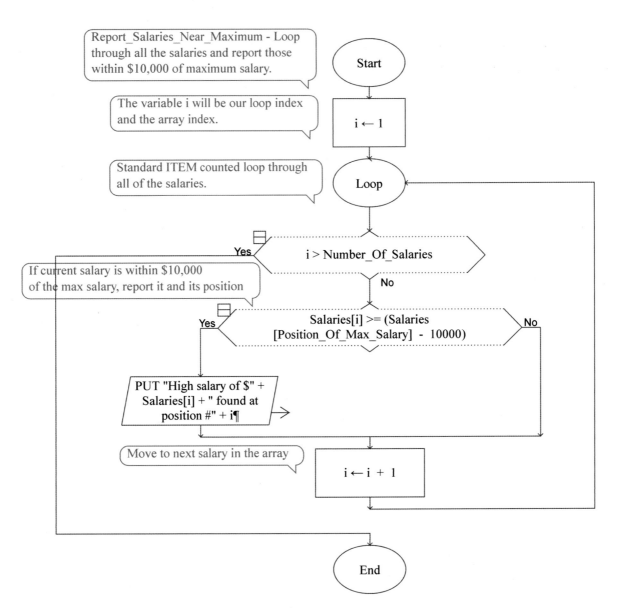

Figure 9-9: Report_Salaries_Near_Maximum Subchart

When testing this algorithm, we would be sure to use test data where the largest salary was at the beginning, middle, and end of the salary inputs. We would also try extreme cases like those with just one salary.

Conclusion

Array variables are a powerful mechanism for storing a group of related values that must be accessed at multiple times in an algorithm. They use a single name for the entire group and an index shown in square brackets to reference individual elements in the group. A variable may be used for this array index. Frequently this array index variable is also the index for a counted loop which allows us to easily traverse through all of the elements in the array.

106

Exercises

1. Write a RAPTOR algorithm that asks the user for a number of scores and then accepts that many input scores putting them into an array. Find the maximum score and count how many scores are within 10, inclusive, of the maximum score. Report the maximum score and the count of scores within 10 of the maximum. Use separate subcharts for input_values, determine_max, and count_within_10_of_max.

2. Write a RAPTOR algorithm that inputs numbers until a negative value is entered. Store the non-negative values into an array. Compute the average of the values and output all the values that are within +/- 5, inclusive, of the average. If there are none in that range, report "None within +/-5 of the average". Use separate subcharts for input_values, calculate_average, and report_within_average_range.

3. Write a RAPTOR algorithm that opens a 600 x 400 graphics window that will display seven balls with centers that have random x coordinates between 50 and 550 and y coordinates equally spaced starting at y=50 and then 100, 150, 200, 250, 300, and 350. Determine the maximum and minimum x coordinates. If a ball's x coordinate is within 100 of the minimum, color it red. If the ball's x coordinate is within 100 of the maximum, color it blue. Otherwise color it yellow. Make appropriate use of sub-charts.

4. **CHALLENGE EXERCISE**: Write a RAPTOR algorithm that accepts 5-digit identification numbers until a value of zero is entered. Any number that is not exactly 5 digits long should be ignored and reported to the Master Console. Then check for duplicate identification numbers reporting the indices of each pair of identical identification numbers. Be sure to report each pair of identical numbers exactly once. For example, if the identification numbers in locations 4 and 17 are the same, report that 4 and 17 are the same, but do not also report that 17 and 4 are the same. *HINT: When nesting counted loops, you can start the index of the inner loop based on the value of the outer loop's index.*

10.   Parallel Arrays: Multiple Collections of Aligned Data

In Chapter 9, we learned how to use array variables to hold groups of related data under one name and use an index to distinguish between the various values held in the array. Sometimes we will have groups of related data with more than one value that we need to save. For example, when processing test scores, we may want to hold both the students' names and their scores while keeping a particular student's name associated with their individual score.

What are Parallel Arrays?

Parallel Arrays offer a great way of doing this. Parallel arrays are two or more arrays each holding data about common objects. The information across the arrays is associated via a common index value.

Consider two arrays holding students' names and test scores, called **Student_Names** and **Scores,** respectively. The elements in the **Student_Names** array would be strings for the names of the students. The elements in the Scores array would be their scores on the test. We would then align the two arrays in parallel so that the name in position 1 of the **Student_Names** array would be associated with that person's score in position 1 of the Scores array. Likewise, the name in **Student_Names[2]** would be that of the student with their test score in **Scores[2]**. The diagram below shows this relationship between the two parallel arrays.

	Student_Names			Scores
1	Joe		1	78
2	Sally		2	89
3	Fred		3	85
4	Gwen		4	96
5	George		5	91

Here the **Student_Names[2]** entry holds "Sally" and **Scores[2]** holds her grade of 89. A similar relationship holds for the other four students where Joe scored a 78, Fred had an 85, Gwen made a 96, and George achieved a 91.

To see how parallel arrays can be used in an algorithm, we use the following example:

> **Student names and test scores are input and then all of those students scoring above the average have their name and score reported.**

The Understand step for this problem is pretty straight forward. The Design step starts with three main tasks:

- Input the names and scores
- Calculate the average score
- Report student names and scores that were above the average

For the Implement Step, the **Main** subchart for this algorithm is shown in Figure 10-1. Note that it calls three subcharts that correspond to these three main tasks of our design.

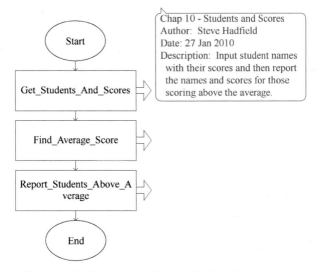

Figure 10-1: Students and Scores Main Subchart

The **Get_Students_And_Scores** subchart is shown in Figure 10-2 and uses a standard ITEM counted loop to input the name and then the score for each of the students in turn. Note that the names and scores are preceded by the number of students so that the algorithm will know how many students there are up front. The Evaluate part of this loop has two Input symbols with the first one obtaining the student name and the second one that student's score. Both are placed directly into the two parallel arrays; **Student_Names** and **Scores**.

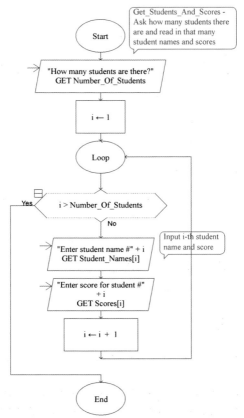

Figure 10-2: Get_Students_And_Scores Subchart

The next task is to determine the average score. The **Find_Average_Score** subchart (Figure 10-3) accomplishes this and is similar to other subcharts that we have already seen.

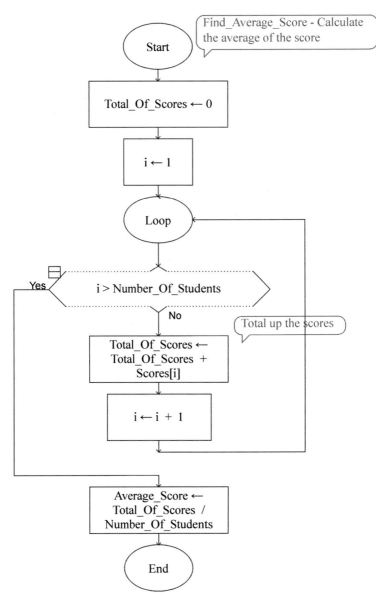

Figure 10-3: Find_Average_Score Subchart

The final subchart, **Report_Students_Above_Average** (shown in Figure 10-4), uses a standard ITEM counted loop to go through all of the test scores in the **Scores** array and compare them to the average held in the **Average_Score** variable that was calculated in the **Find_Average_Score** subchart. When an above average score is found, both the student's name and their score are reported.

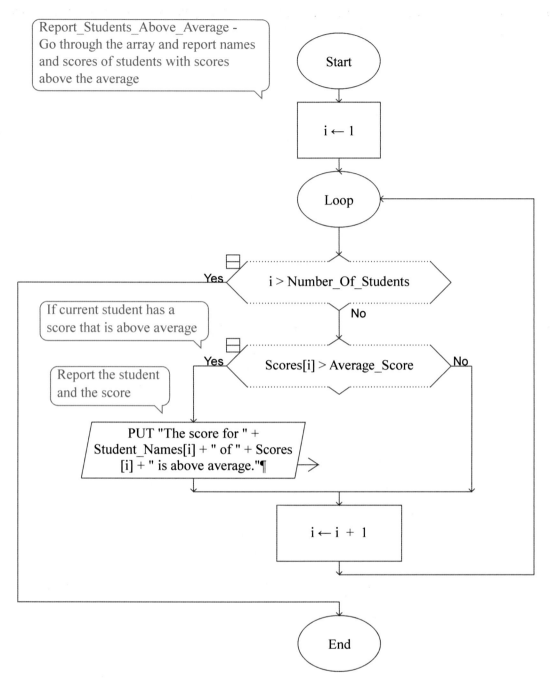

Figure 10-4: Report_Students_Above_Average Subchart

111

Example Problem – Multiple Bouncing Balls

Now that we have a basic understanding of parallel arrays, we will work another example problem that requires them. Our problem statement is:

> **Create an animation where the user specifies the initial location of multiple randomly colored balls via left mouse clicks. A right mouse click signals the end of adding balls and starts them moving in random directions bouncing off of the walls until a key is pressed to end the animation.**

A sample run of this algorithm would produce a display that looks like the image in Figure 10-5.

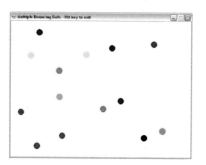

Figure 10-5: Sample Display for Multiple Bouncing Balls

Extracting the key points from this problem statement for the Understand Step, we come up with the inputs, processing tasks, outputs, and variables shown in Table 10-1. Reviewing the table, we realize that we have about all the information required to develop our list of tasks (for the Design step).

Table 10-1: Multiple Bouncing Balls Input-Process-Output with Variables

Inputs	Processing	Outputs	Variables

• Left mouse clicks to place balls
• Right mouse click to signal end of input and to start the animation
• Any key hit to exit
	• Obtain ball locations randomly setting color and movement
	• Run the animations moving and bouncing balls around the window
	• Terminate animation
		• Balls draw in initial locations
		• Balls moving about the window
			• Parallel arrays for
			  o Ball X coordinates
			  o Ball Y coordinates
			  o Ball colors
			  o Ball X change
			  o Ball Y change
			• Number of balls

Using our table to develop a List of Tasks, we come up with the following top level tasks:

- Set up graphics window with title
- Place balls per user left clicks
- Set up animation with screen directions
- Loop through animation using Erase scene – Move objects – Draw scene
- Close graphics window

By adding details to our list of top level tasks to elaborate our design, we end up with:

- Set up graphics window with title
- Place balls per user left clicks
  - Loop through getting ball locations until a right mouse click
    - Set ball X and Y coordinates per left mouse click location
    - Set color randomly; taking care to not color a ball with background color
    - Set ball's movement with random X change and Y change values
- Set up animation with screen directions
- Loop through animation using Erase scene – Move objects – Draw scene
  - Move balls by looping through and adding X and Y changes and handling bounces
  - Draw balls by looping through them drawing them in their new locations
- Close graphics window

The List of Variables contains the **Number_Of_Balls** variable plus five parallel arrays which are **Ball_X** for the X positions of the balls, **Ball_Y** for the Y positions, **Ball_Color** for the colors of the balls, **Ball_X_Change** for the movements in the X direction, and **Ball_Y_Change** for movement in the Y direction.

The Main flowchart, implemented based upon the List of Tasks for our design, is shown in Figure 10-6. Calls are made to the built-in RAPTOR graphics procedures; **Open_Graph_Window**, **Set_Window**, **Freeze_Graph_Window**, **Clear_ Window**, **Update_Graph_Window**, **Unfreeze_Graph_Window**, and **Close_Graph_Window** to implement a smooth flowing graphics animation as we learned in Chapter 8.

The **Place_Balls** subchart uses the **Number_Of_Balls** variable to track how many balls the user has placed. A Loop construct that exits with a right mouse click controls the placement of the balls. A Selection construct checks if there was a left mouse click. If so, the number of balls is incremented, the mouse click location is used to set the ball's location, a random color is generated (and updated if there is a conflict with the background color), the initial direction for the ball is set, and then the ball is drawn as feedback to the user.

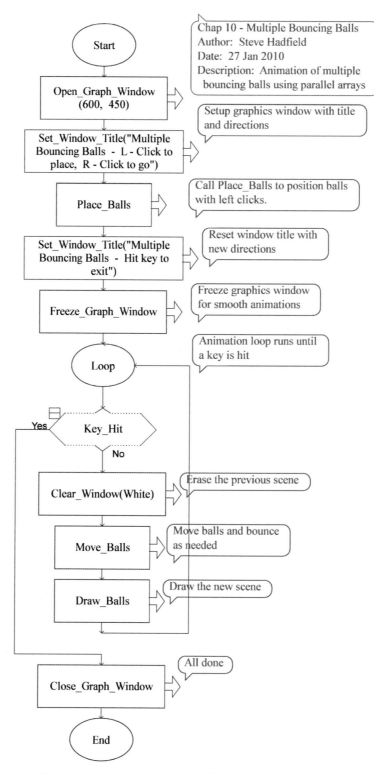

Figure 10-6: Multiple Bouncing Balls Main Subchart

114

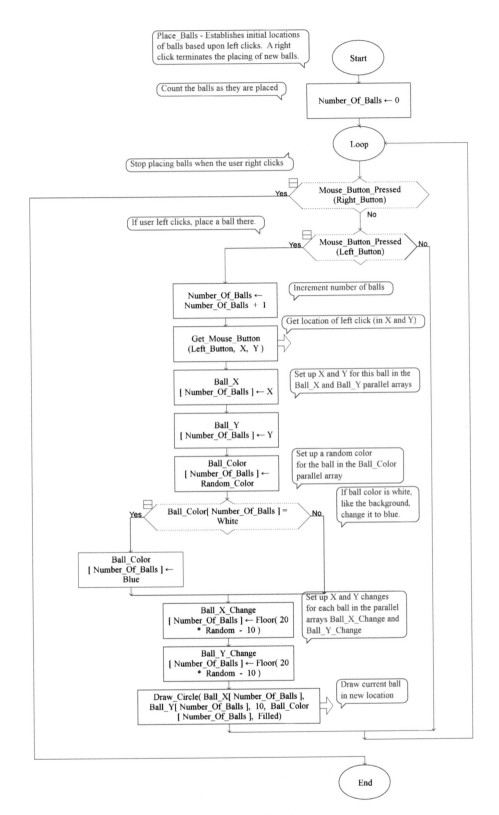

Figure 10-7: Place_Balls Subchart

115

The **Move_Balls** subchart, in Figure 10-8, uses a standard ITEM counted loop to go through each of the balls (one-at-a-time) and updates their locations using the **Ball_X**, **Ball_Y**, **Ball_X_Change**, and **Ball_Y_Change** parallel arrays.

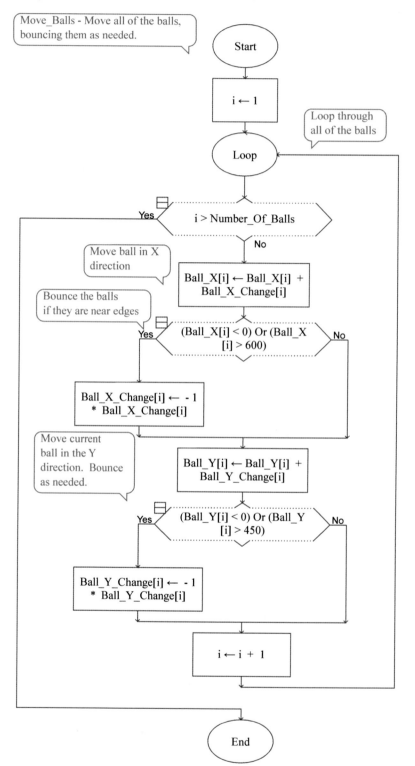

Figure 10-8: Move_Balls Subchart

116

The **Draw_Balls** subchart (shown in Figure 10-9) also uses a standard ITEM counted loop to traverse through all of the balls and draw them in their newly updated **Ball_X** and **Ball_Y** location. A call to **Delay_For** paces the speed of the animation. The **Update_Graph_Window** call displays the updated scene with all of the repositioned balls to produce a smooth animation.

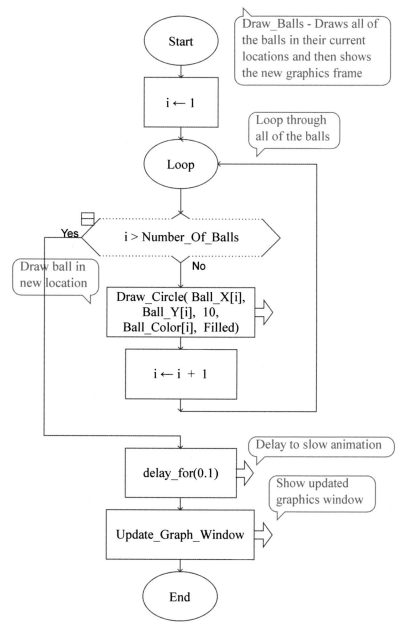

Figure 10-9: Draw_Balls Subchart

Conclusion

Array Variables provide an efficient means for storing a group of related variables using a common name for the group and an index to access individual members of the group. When there are multiple groups of data that are related, we can align distinct arrays by their indexed positions so the same index value can be used across different arrays to access all information for an entity. We saw how this was done for student names and scores as well as the locations, colors, and movements of a set of balls in an animation. The use of parallel arrays greatly expands the set of problems that we can address with RAPTOR and allows us to do so efficiently using the standard ITEM counted loop.

Exercises

1. Write a RAPTOR algorithm that asks the user for a number of actors and then repeatedly accept the name and number of films the actor has been in storing the names and numbers in parallel arrays. Then calculate the average number of films these actors have been in and report the names for each actor that was in the average number of films or more. Use separate sub-charts for getting the information, computing the average number of films, and reporting the names of the actors with the average number of films or more.

2. Write a RAPTOR algorithm that accepts the names of countries and their per capita spending on education (in US dollars) into separate arrays until "END" is entered for a country name. Determine average and maximum per capita education spending amounts. Then count how many countries are at or above the average per capita education spending. Finally, report the names of all the countries that are within $100 of the maximum per capita education spending amount. Use separate sub-charts such that no sub-chart has more than one loop in it.

3. Write a RAPTOR algorithm that accepts the names of cities, their average annual precipitation, and average annual temperature until "STOP" is entered for city name. Calculate the average, minimum, and maximum values for precipitation and temperature. Report the names of all cities that are within +/- 10 degrees of the average temperature and are within 5 inches of the maximum annual precipitation. If no cities met these criteria, report "No cities meet criteria". Use separate sub-charts such that no sub-chart has more than one loop in it.

4. Adapt the Multiple Bouncing Balls algorithm to move multiple UFOs across a scenic background.

5. Enhance your Exercise 4 program so that instead of bouncing off the edges, UFOs wrap-around to the other side. For example, those going off of the right side, appear on the left side and those going off the top edge, appear at the bottom edge.

6. Write a RAPTOR algorithm that asks the user for the number of balls to bounce around a graphics window. Create that many balls all with the same size radius and each in its own random (x, y) location moving in its own random direction and bouncing off the walls. All but the last ball with have an initial color of Blue. The last ball will be red. As the balls bounce around, check for collisions between any pair of balls. If any red ball collides with a blue ball, the blue ball will change to red. When all of the balls become red, stop the animation in place and wait for the use to left-click the mouse to signal that the program should terminate and close the graphics windows. Two balls 'collide' when the distance between their center (x, y) points is less than the sum of their radii. Use separate sub-charts so that each sub-chart has no more than one loop, except for the one which checks for collisions which may have one loop nested within another.

11. Two-Dimensional Arrays: Multidimensional Groupings of Data

In the last chapter, we learned about how multiple arrays could be used in parallel with entries at the same index in the different arrays being associated together. The example had student names in one array (the array named "Student_Names") and scores in a separate array (named "Scores"). The entry Student_Names[2] contained the name of student #2 and the Scores[2] entry contained the score for that person; Sally in the example provided as Figure 11-1. This clever use of two arrays let us put together two pieces of information, Sally's name and her score, by aligning them at the same index value (2 in this case) of the two arrays.

	Student_Names		Scores
1	Joe	1	78
2	Sally	2	89
3	Fred	3	85
4	Gwen	4	96
5	George	5	91

Figure 11-1: Parallel 1D Arrays for Students and Scores

But what if there were more tests, say three distinct tests?

We certainly could have more parallel arrays; one for the student names and then three more for each of the individual tests. This is a very reasonable and workable solution. However, with each additional test we would need to go back and add or modify a significant number of symbols in our program to deal with the additional arrays.

Another approach would be to use a two-dimensional array where rows correspond to students and columns correspond to test such as is shown in Figure 11-2.

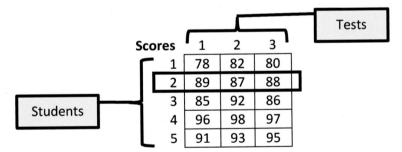

Figure 11-2: 2D Array with Rows for Students and Columns for Tests

Details of Two-Dimensional Arrays

The two-dimensional array Scores requires two indices; one indicating the row and the other identifying the column. For example (from Figure 11-2), the reference, **Scores[2,3]**, refers to the entry in the second row and third column which is 88. This entry means that student #2 on test #3 scored 88.

Recall that with one-dimensional arrays, as shown in Figure 11-3, we had an array name, an array index, and the value, where the value is what is held in the array at the given index (position). The array element, such as **Scores[2]**, is how we got to a specific value in the array.

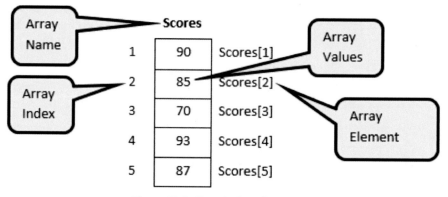

Figure 11-3: Description of a 1D Array

Now with two-dimensional arrays, we have an array name, a row index, a column index, and the value, where the value is what is held in the array at the row specified by the row index and the column specified by the column index. Array references, such as **Scores[2, 3]**, now contain two numbers inside the square brackets: the row index and the column index. Figure 11-4 shows this relationship.

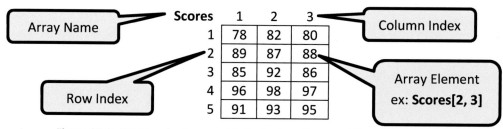

Figure 11-4: 2D Array for Scores with Students as Rows and Tests as Columns

The use of both row and column indices can be a bit confusing at first. To help ensure that we have a handle on these, Figure 11-5 shows how each one of the values in our two-dimensional **Scores** array is referenced.

Scores	1	2	3
1	Scores[1,1]	Scores[1,2]	Scores[1,3]
2	Scores[2,1]	Scores[2,2]	Scores[2,3]
3	Scores[3,1]	Scores[3,2]	Scores[3,3]
4	Scores[4,1]	Scores[4,2]	Scores[4,3]
5	Scores[5,1]	Scores[5,2]	Scores[5,3]

Figure 11-5: 2D Array for Scores with Indexing Shown

One of the many really nice features with RAPTOR is that arrays can grow as needed. This was the case with one-dimensional arrays. If we had a one dimensional array of four elements named Scores and needed to add a fifth score, we would just put **Scores[5]** and we had a fifth array element.

The same applies to two-dimensional arrays. If we state **Scores[5, 3]**, RAPTOR will either create a new array with five rows and three columns if this is first mention of the Scores array, or, if the Scores already exists of a smaller size, it will be extended with the necessary rows and/or columns with any added elements taking the value of zero.

For example, if the Scores array does not yet exist, the assignment: **Scores[5, 3] ← 95** would produce the array shown in Figure 11-6.

Scores	1	2	3
1	0	0	0
2	0	0	0
3	0	0	0
4	0	0	0
5	0	0	95

Figure 11-6: 2D Array for Scores for Five Students (Rows) and Three Tests (Columns)

If the Scores array on the left side of Figure 11-7 already existed, **Scores[5, 3] ← 95** would produce the array on the right side of that figure.

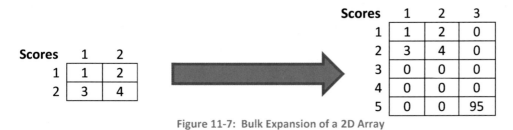

Figure 11-7: Bulk Expansion of a 2D Array

Traversing Through a Two-Dimensional Array

When we first started to talk about arrays (the one-dimensional variety), we quickly realized that we could use a variable for the index and then use an **ITEM** (**I**nitialize-**T**est-**E**valuate-**M**odify) loop structure to go through (traverse) each of the entries in the array. That ITEM loop structure for traversing a one-dimensional array looked like the example in Figure 11-8.

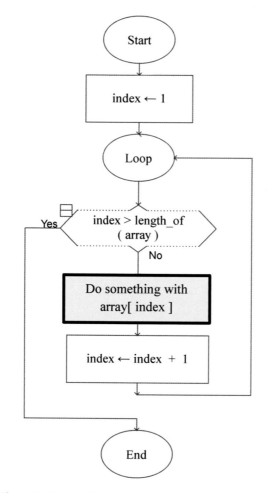

Figure 11-8: Loop for Traversing a 1D Array

When we need to traverse through two-dimensional arrays, we will use this same ITEM loop approach, but we will need two loops; one for going through the rows and a separate one for the columns. Importantly, we can "nest" one loop inside of the other to get at every entry. The two common ways of doing this are:

1. By rows and then each column within the row.
   a. To do this, the outer loop is on the row index and the inner loop is on the column index.
   b. Figure 11-9 shows this approach.
   c. Figure 11-10 shows the nested ITEM loops to accomplish this.

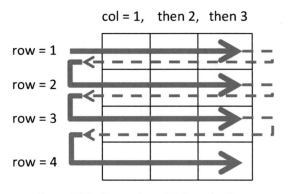

col = 1, then 2, then 3

row = 1

row = 2

row = 3

row = 4

Figure 11-9: Traversing a 2D Array by Rows

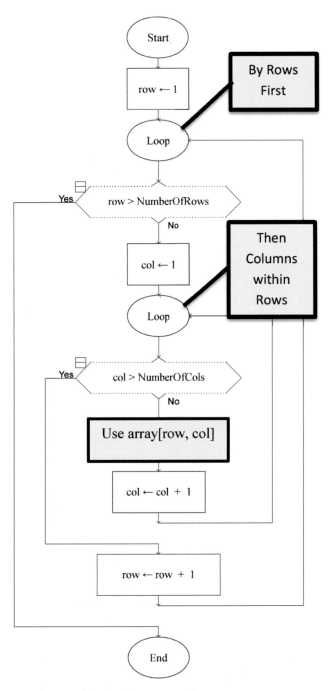

Figure 11-10: By Rows, and then Columns Nested Loops

2. By columns and then each row within a column.
   a. To do this, the outer loop is on the column index and the inner loop is on the row index.
   b. Figure 11-11 shows this approach.
   c. Figure 11-12 shows the nested ITEM loops to accomplish this.

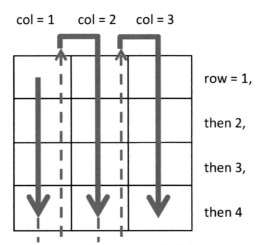

col = 1   col = 2   col = 3

row = 1,

then 2,

then 3,

then 4

Figure 11-11: Traversing a 2D Array by Columns

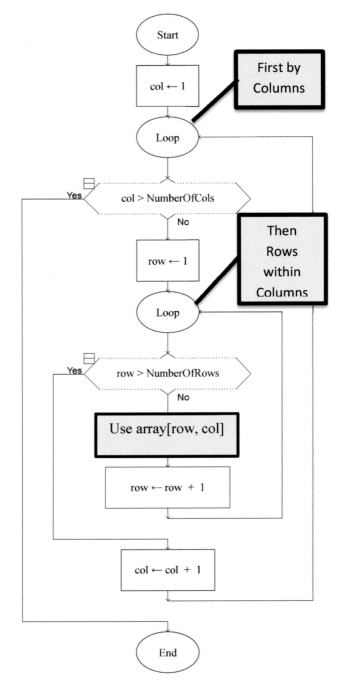

Figure 11-12: By Columns, and then Rows Nested Loops

When we nest loops to traverse a two-dimensional (2D) array, we need to take care to reset the index of the inner loop each time we go through the outer loop. For example, when traversing by rows, the inner loop must reset the **col** variable to 1 each time before the inner column loop runs.

To better understand how we can use 2D arrays and row / column traversals, let us look at example that builds upon on handling of student test scores. Specifically, we will input student names and their scores on a number of tests. Then we will calculate and report the average for each student, the average for each test, and a count of how many students passed each test.

Our **List of Tasks** (for the start of the Design step) will be as follows:

- Input names and test scores for all students
- Calculate students' averages
- Calculate test averages
- Count how many passed each test

We will need two arrays for this. The first array is a 1D array that holds each student's name. The second array will hold the each student's scores on each test and will thus need to be a 2D array. In both arrays, rows will correspond to students. In the second array, columns will correspond to the individual tests. The separate 1D array for student names is needed because the names are all strings; whereas the scores are all numbers. The Figure 11-13 illustrates these two arrays.

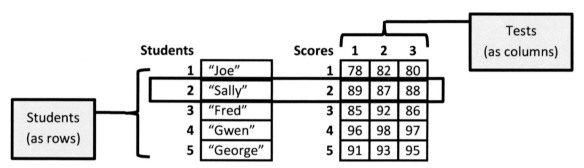

Figure 11-13: Arrays for Student Scores Algorithm

Note that we are using Students as a parallel array where the Students array index is also used as a row index for the Scores array. The column index in the Scores array distinguishes the different tests, in this case three of them.

In this example, Students[2] refers to the name "Sally" and Scores[2,1], Scores[2,2], and Scores [2,3] refer to her scores on each of the three tests.

Following an incremental design-implement-test strategy, we will consider each main task one-at-a-time and creating its List of Tasks design, coding the subchart, and testing it. These subcharts would need to be called from Main and additional logic would be needed to report the results; it would be best to make these separate subcharts as well. These remaining subcharts are left for you to implement in Exercise 1. The Main subchart of our implementation is shown in Figure 11-14.

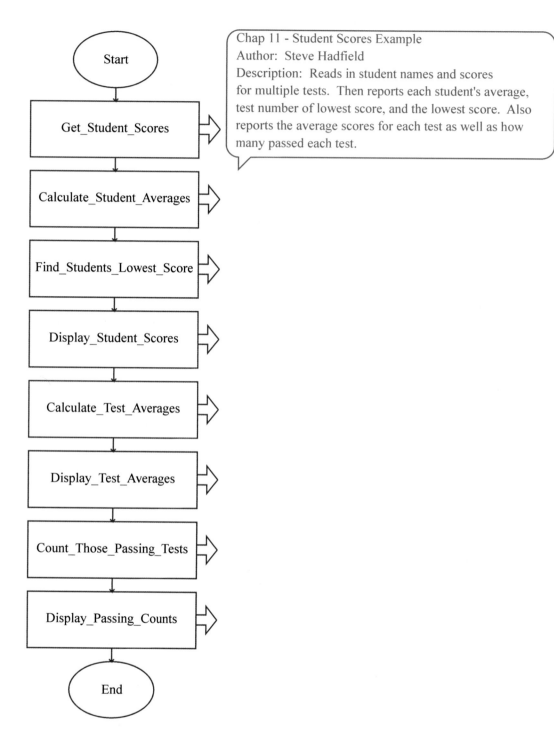

Figure 11-14: Student Scores Main Subchart

Get_Student_Scores: This subchart will ask the user for the number students and the number of tests so that our program can handle varying numbers of students and tests. We will use a row (student-based) traversal for getting the student names and test scores from the user. The Get_Student_Scores subchart is shown as Figure 11-15.

126

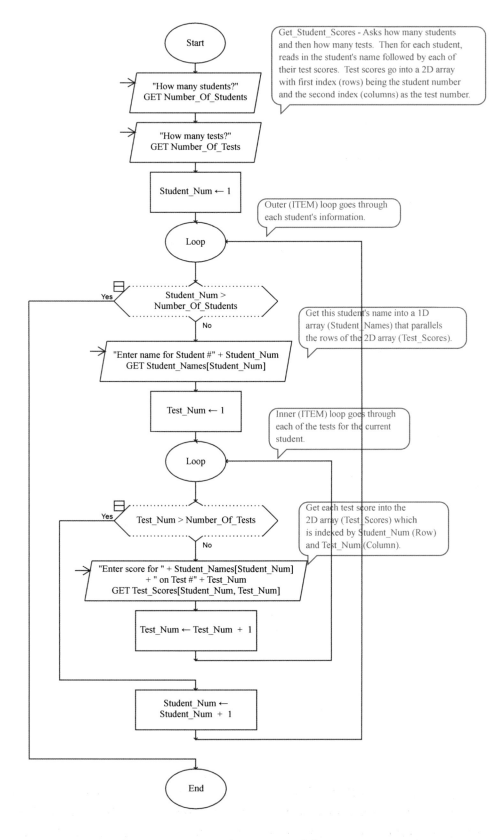

Figure 11-15: Get_Student_Scores Subchart

127

Calculate Student Averages: To calculate student averages, we will use another row-based traversal with the outer loop taking us through each student and the inner loop through each student's tests. Inside the student outer loop we will need to reset our Total_Test_Scores accumulating variable to zero. See Figure 11-16 for the Calculate_Student_Averages subchart.

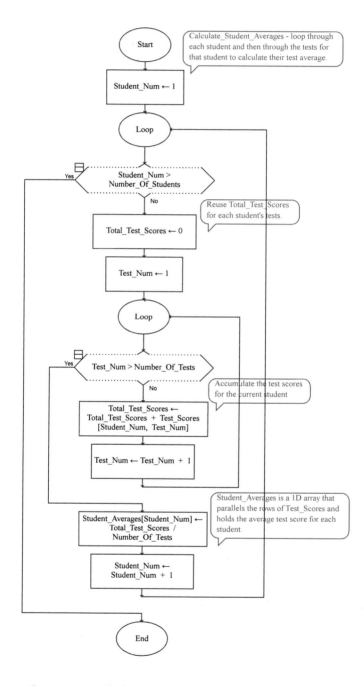

Figure 11-16: Calculate_Student_Averages Subchart

Calculate Test Averages: To calculate the average for each test, we will need to traverse the Scores array by columns (test-based).   The averages for each test go into a separate 1D array called **Test_Averages**. This array can then be used in a variety of ways to include reporting the test averages. Figure 11-17 shows the Calculate_Test_Averages subchart.

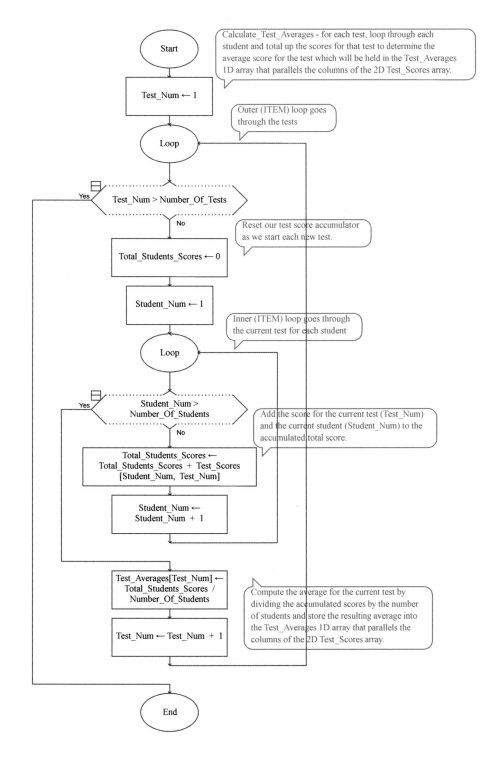

Figure 11-17: Calculate_Test_Averages Subchart

129

Count Those Passing Tests: Finally, we can traverse the Scores array again by columns (test-based) to count how many students passed each test (achieved a score of 70 or better). These counts are stored in a 1D array called **Test_Passing_Student_Counts**. See Figure 11-18 for the details of this subchart.

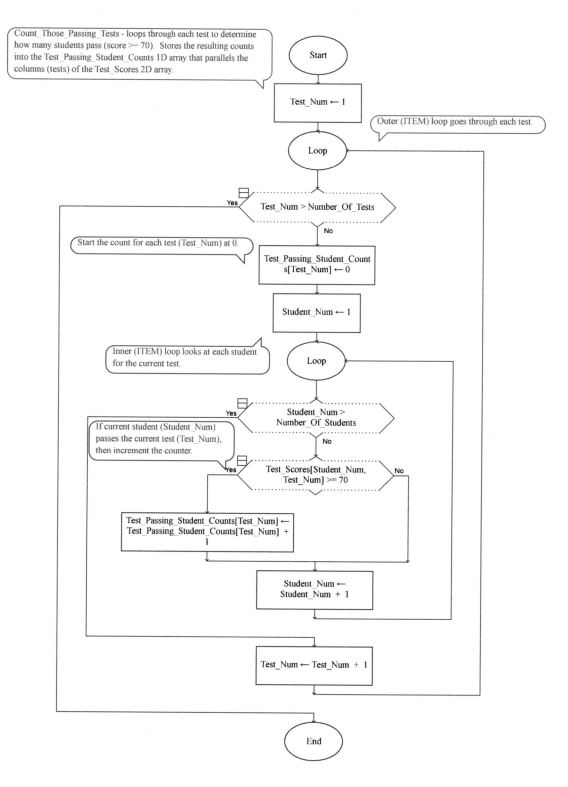

Figure 11-18: Count_Those_Passing_Tests Subchart

Tic-Tac-Toe Example

In the preceding student score example, we saw that 2D arrays can be very useful for storing and organizing data. We also saw how nested loops help us to traverse a 2D array by rows or columns as needed for the task at hand.

Another common use of 2D arrays is to model a game or simulation. The model is the set of values (typically numeric) that represent the current game board or status of the simulation. Our program uses the model to keep track of and manipulate the game or simulation. Corresponding to the model is the "view" which is how the user sees the current game board or simulation status. The view is typically shown using a graphics window. Our program will update the view based upon the current state of the model.

For our second 2D array example, we will begin the implementation of a Tic-Tac-Toe game using a 2D array for the model of the game and then a graphics window for the user's view of the game. The Figure 11-19 shows the relationship between the model and the view. Note, we are showing the array with its row indices reverse which is a bit curious, if not outright weird. However, we will see how thinking of the array in this manner will help with mapping between the model's array and the view's grid because the RAPTOR graphics window has y values that start with zero at the bottom and get larger as we go up. If we think of the array's row indices as getting bigger as we go up, then the mapping becomes easier.

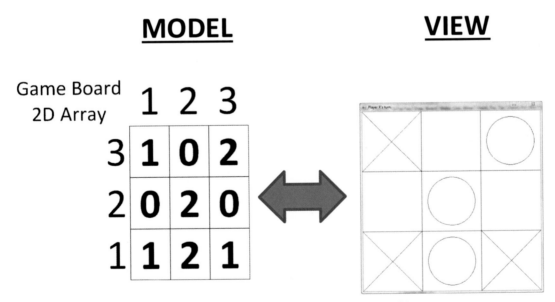

Figure 11-19: Model-View Relationship

Within the model, the state of the game is represented with numbers where a zero represents an empty cell, one (1) represents an 'X', and two (2) represents an 'O'. Compare the values in the model's 2D Game Board array to the view on the right which is how the player will see the state of the game.

In addition to the 2D Game Board array, our Tic-Tac-Toe program will need some additional variables to keep track of things such as which player's turn it is and whether or not the game is over.

With this understanding of how the model and view of our game will work together, let us start to build our game.

For the Understand step, we develop the Input-Process-Output with Variables summary shown in Table 11-1.

Table 11-1: Input-Process-Output with Variables for Tic-Tac-Toe

Inputs	Processing	Outputs	Variables
• User's placement of their next mark	• Initialize game • Draw the gameboard • Handle user's move • Update gameboard • Check for tie (full gameboard) • Check for a win • Conclude the game	• Win / tie message	• 2D array for the game model • Current player

The Design step starts with the following List of Top-Level Tasks:

- Initialize the Tic-Tac-Toe game.
- Draw the initial gameboard.
- Loop
    - Get the current user's move.
    - Draw the updated gameboard.
    - Check for a tie (full gameboard).
    - Check for a win.
    - Exit loop if the game is over
- End loop
- Conclude the game with an appropriate message.

The Implement step begins with the Main subchart creating calls to the necessary lower-level subcharts and putting in the appropriate control structures. The resulting Main flowchart is shown in Figure 11-20.

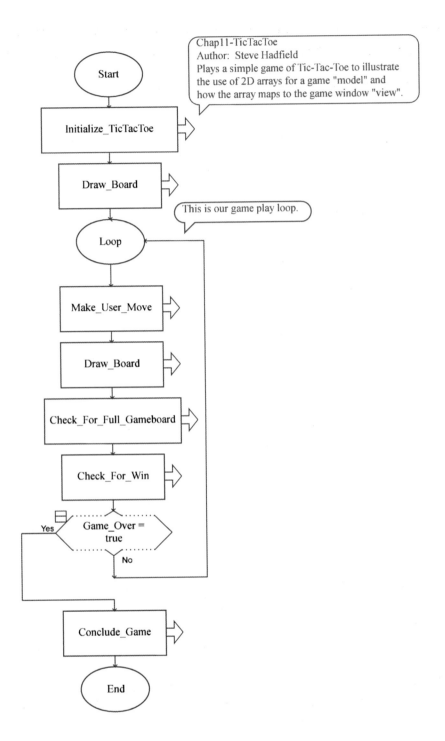

Figure 11-20: Main Subchart for the Tic-Tac-Toe Game

This Main flowchart illustrates a fairly typical game program organization. First the state (model) for the game is initialized and the initial view is established. Next, the game play loop repeats the steps and checks of the game until the game ends. Finally, the game concludes with a display of the game's results. Within the game play loop we have calls to four subcharts to handle the user making moves, displaying the resulting state of the game (updating the view based upon the updated model), checking for a full gameboard (all cells filled), and checking for a win.

From here we iterate through incremental additions (frequently called "spirals") to our program taking each main-level subchart and accomplishing a full Understand-Design-Implement-Test cycle on it. But before we dive too far into that, we should plan out an intelligent ordering of what to do as some pieces need to be complete before we can do others. We call this a "Spiral Development Plan". For our Tic-Tac-Toe game, we might use the Spiral Development Plan below:

Spiral Development Plan for the Tic-Tac-Toe Game

1. Create the Main subchart with calls to the appropriate subcharts (that at this point are empty – we call these "stubs") (Spiral 1).
2. Understand-Design-Implement-Test the Initialize_TicTacToe subchart (Spiral 2).
3. Understand-Design-Implement-Test the Draw_Board subchart (Spiral 3).
4. Understand-Design-Implement-Test the Make_User_Move subchart – checking that moves are shown in the View and represented in the Model using the Debug window in RAPTOR (Spiral 4).
5. Understand-Design-Implement-Test the Check_For_Win subchart (Spiral 5).
6. Understand-Design-Implement-Test the Conclude_Game subchart (Spiral 6).
7. Understand-Design-Implement-Test the Check_For_Full_Gameboard subchart (Spiral 7).
8. Conduct full testing of the entire program.

In what follows, we will focus on initializing the game (the Initialize_TicTacToe subchart), updating the view based upon the model (the Draw_Board subchart), and handling the user making moves (the Make_User_Move subchart). The remaining subcharts will be left as exercises for the reader.

Initialize_TicTacToe: The **Game_Board** 2D array provides the model that represents our gameboard. All entries are set to zero to indicate empty cells. The model also includes the **Current_Player**, **Game_Over**, and **Winning_Player** variables to track the state of the game. In addition to setting the values of the model, this subchart creates the **Window_Size** and **Cell_Size** variables to control the appearance of the view and then creates the graphics window for the view and draws the grid of cells. The **Msg_To_User** variable will be used by the **Draw_Board** to display information and instructions to the user in the window title area of the graphics window view. Read through the symbols and comments of the Initialize_TicTacToe subchart shown as Figure 11-21 to understand the details.

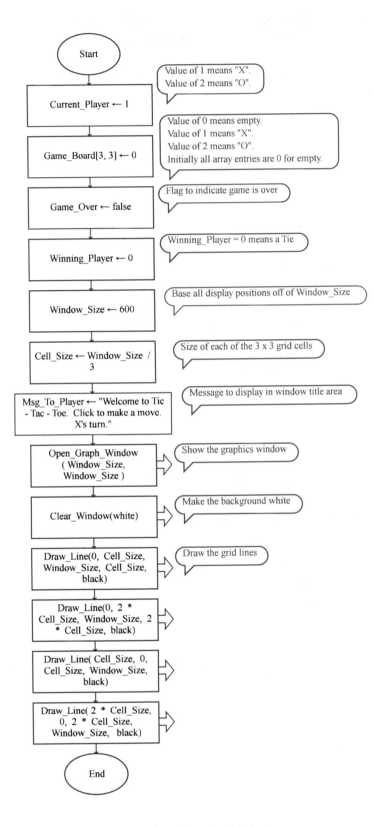

Figure 11-21: Initialize_TicTacToe Subchart

135

Draw_Board: This subchart (Figure 11-22) displays the **Msg_To_Player** string to the graphics window title area to provide information and instructions to the user. Then a traversal of the **Game_Board** 2D array allows displaying of each entry in the array to the view provided by the graphics window. This process involves some arithmetic as the **row** and **col** index variables are multiplied by **Cell_Size** to obtain the correct positions of the cell's corners within the graphics window view. Note that **Cell_Size * (col - 1)** gives the x value of the cell's left side, whereas **Cell_Size * col** gives the x value of the right side. Vertically, **Cell_Size * (row - 1)** gives the y value of the cell bottoml and **Cell_Size * row** gives the y value of the cell's top. For the O's, we find the center of the cell and use **Cell_Size * 0.4** to get an appropriate radius.

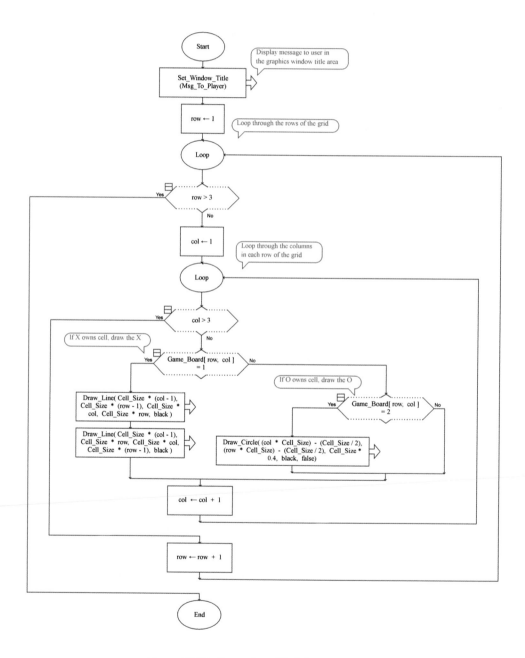

Figure 11-22: Draw_Board Subchart

136

Make_User_Move: Within the **Make_User_Move** subchart (Figure 11-23), a call to **Get_Mouse_Button** retrieves the location of the user's click as (**Mouse_X**, **Mouse_Y**) which must then be translated to the corresponding indices into the **Game_Board** 2D array. This translation is done as follows:

Selected_Row ← Floor((Mouse_Y / Cell_Size) + 1

Selected_Col ← Floor((Mouse_X / Cell_Size) + 1

The corresponding location in the **Game_Board** 2D array is checked. If empty, then the move can be made and that entry in the **Game_Board** array is updated to the **Current_Player** indicating a successful move. The **Current_Player** is then changed to the other player and the **Msg_To_Player** string is updated appropriately. If the user's click was in an already filled cell, the click is ignored and **Msg_To_Player** takes on an appropriate message for the user.

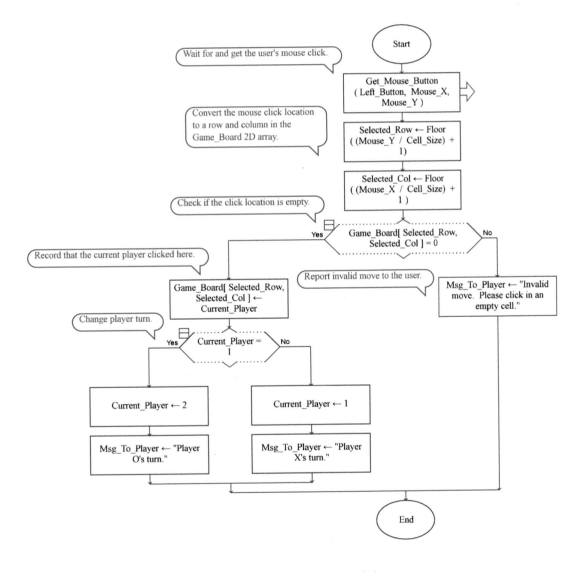

Figure 11-23: Make_User_Move Subchart

As mentioned earlier, the remaining subcharts for Tic-Tac-Toe are left as exercises. To help with these subcharts consider the following hints:

Check_For_Full_Gameboard:

- Set the Game_Over variable to true.
- Traverse through the rows and columns of the Game_Board array. If any array entry represents an empty cell, set the Game_Over variable back to false.

Check_For_Win:

- Check all three entries on the main diagonal for being equal to each other.
- Check all three entries on the opposing diagonal for being equal to each other.
- Check all three entries for each row. Best to use a loop for doing this.
- Check all three entries for each column. Best to use a loop to do this as well.
- For any of these checks, make sure they are not all empty. If they are not all empty but they are all the same, you have a winner so record that in the Winning_Player variable and set Game_Over to true.

Conclude_Game:

- If Winning_Player is zero, you have a tie. Otherwise, Winning_Player = 1 means X wins and 2 means O wins.
- Output an appropriate message centered in the graphics window. Would be good to make it a bigger font size and a different font color. Consider using the RAPTOR Set_Font_Size(), Get_Font_Width, Get_Font_Height, Get_Window_Width, and Get_Window_Height calls and functions to help with sizing and centering the final message.
- Provide user instructions in the graphics window title area.
- Wait for a mouse click or key press and then close the graphics window.

Mapping Between the Model and View

As mentioned earlier, the use of a model based upon a 2D array and a corresponding grid-based view makes for nice way to implement many different games and can also be used for a variety of simulations. The mapping of entries between the model's 2D array and the view's grid can get a bit tricky so we will look at this in a bit more detail. The idea here is to map the row and column indices for the model's array to (x, y) positions in the view's grid and vice versa. Perhaps somewhat counter intuitively the row index actually maps to the y component of location in the view's grid and the column index maps to the x component. To understand this mapping better consider Figure 11-24 which illustrates the mapping between a 3 x 3 model array and a 600 x 600 view grid (giving a cell size of 200 x 200 as 600 / 3 = 200).

MODEL'S ARRAY   VIEW'S GRID

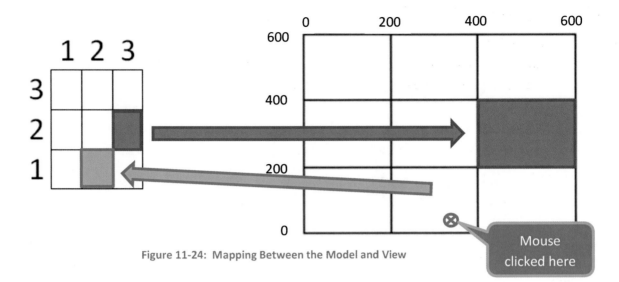

Figure 11-24: Mapping Between the Model and View

First, we will map from the model's array row and column indices to the (x, y) locations in the view's grid. For this, take row = 2 and column = 3 as shown with the blue rectangles and arrow in the figure above. The mappings would be as follows:

Row Index to Y Position

Top Y: $y \leftarrow$ Cell_Size * row   (which is 400 $\leftarrow$ 200 * 2)

Bottom Y: $y \leftarrow$ Cell_Size * (row-1)   (which is 200 $\leftarrow$ 200 * (2-1))

Column Index to X Position

Right X: $x \leftarrow$ Cell_Size * col   (which is 600 $\leftarrow$ 200 * 3)

Left X: $x \leftarrow$ Cell_Size * (col-1)   (which is 400 $\leftarrow$ 200 * (3-1))

Mapping the other way we take an (x, y) location in the view's grid such as x = 325 and y = 150 and show how it maps to row = 1 and column = 2 entry in the model's array as shown with green in the figure above.

Y Position to Row Index

Row Index: row $\leftarrow$ Floor((y / Cell_Size) + 1)

which is   1 $\leftarrow$ Floor((150 / 200) + 1) as (150 / 200) + 1 is 1.75 and 1 $\leftarrow$ Floor(1.75)

139

X Position to Column Index

Column Index: col ← Floor ((x / Cell_Size) + 1)

which is 2 ← Floor((325 / 200) + 1) as (325 / 200) + 1 is 2.625 and 2 ← Floor(2.625)

Conclusion

In this chapter, we explored the extension of the array to a second dimension which allowed the data stored in the array to be organized both as rows and columns. In our first example of students and their scores, the Scores 2D array related rows to students and the columns to distinct tests. These 2D arrays can be traversed either by row or column which provide great flexibility for computing various results.

Next, we introduced the idea of a model and view approach to game design where the model relied on a 2D array to keep track of and manipulate the state of the game and the view provides a representation of the game state for the user. Formulae for mapping between the model and view provided a basis for both presenting the state of the game and accepting user inputs via the view (graphics window).

Exercises

1. Complete the Student Scores for Multiple Tests example in a step-wise manner (each subsequent step relies on the earlier steps) as follows:

    a. Include subcharts for displaying student averages, test averages, and counts of those passing each test as well as a Main subchart to call the other subcharts.

    b. Add additional capabilities to determine the highest score on each test. Report that highest score and the student that received that highest score. If more than one student achieved the highest score, you could either report just the first, the last, or all of the students' names.

    c. Count how many students are within 10 points (inclusive) of the highest score on each test.

2. **Patriotic Squares**: Create a 300 x 300 graphics window and divide it evenly into a 3 x 3 grid. Color each cell in the grid initially as white. When the user clicks in a cell the first time, change the color to red. When the user clicks in a cell the second time, change the color to blue. Ignore any subsequent clicks in a cell. Hint: for your model, use a 3 x 3 array with each entry corresponding to a cell in the grid. Use numbers in the array to indicate the color to use for the subsequent grid cell (i.e. 0 for white, 1 for red, and 2 for blue).

    a. Further extend your Patriotic Squares game by asking the user for the size of your grid and have your program automatically adjust the number and size of grid cells.

    b. Use other colors and store them in an array indexed by the number of clicks. You might have more than three colors and even use randomly generated colors which are set upon program start up to make things more interesting.

3. **Tic-Tac-Toe**: Complete the Tic-Tac-Toe example begun in this chapter to include checking for full board (**Check_For_Full_Gameboard** subchart) and wins (**Check_For_Win** subchart) and concluding the game (**Conclude_Game** subchart). You may want to review the hints for these subcharts which were provided earlier in the reading.

4. **Challenge Problem - Checkers**: Implement a game of checkers using an 8 x 8 gameboard based upon the model / view approach described in this chapter. Consider using the following progression for your implementation:

   a. Create a subchart to draw the checker board in an already open graphics window. A trick that you can use here to generate the correct pattern is to evaluate **(row + col) rem 2**. If the row + col sum is even this expression will evaluate zero. If it is odd, then the expression evaluates to one. Use a selection to check if this expression is zero and use one color if this is the case. Otherwise use the other color.

   b. Create a 2D array for the model much like you did for Tic-Tac-Toe where a zero (0) entry indicates empty, a one (2) indicates the first player, and a two (2) indicates the second player. Initialize this array so that it contains the initial placement of the chips. Then draw the checker board with the chips on the board.

   c. Add a game play loop to the Main subchart and a subchart for handling user moves. Recommend you move chips with two clicks; one click to select the chip and a second click to place the chip. Note you will have to make sure the player clicks a cell that has her chip on the first click and a cell that is open on the second click. These checks are sufficient for now but you will improve upon then in the next step. As an alternative to the two-click more technique, you could do a drag-and-drop approach.

   d. Add the ability to jump and capture the other player's chips. Take care to handle the edges of the board and only allow valid jumps. Would be good to improve the overall move checking at this point as well so the player can only move to valid open positions. Single jumps at this point will be fine. You might consider adding a score keeping mechanism that reports the number of captured chips for each player. This would be a good time to check for wins. Note, it is possible to "tie" where neither player has a move but both players have chips on the board.

   e. Next you might consider supporting multiple jumps. For this, you will want to allow the player to either take or not take opportunities for multiple jumps (and they may not even realize that they have a multiple jump opportunity). One way to handle this is to add an "end turn" button which must be pressed to conclude the current player's turn and give the other player their turn.

   f. If you really want a challenge, you can add the possibility for chips to become Kings. There are additional rules and features for the Game of Checkers which can be implemented. See http://boardgames.about.com/cs/checkersdraughts/ht/play_checkers.htm.

Made in the USA
Monee, IL
29 November 2022

18837669R00090